What peop

Integrated Busines .ing

Integrated Business To Business Marketing by Philip Allott offers a refreshing take on the latest developments in the UK. Easy read that makes technical subjects such as search engine optimisation easy to understand and follow for any practitioner. Aimed at small and medium sized enterprises, budget focused tactics and thinking tools are used to help in managing marketing resources in an effective way. This book makes core references to practical tools which help in creating a marketing strategy which will last.

Aleksej Heinze, Associate Professor at Kedge Business School, France

This book is a must read for anyone wanting to better understand the relationship between integrated marketing and business growth. Presented in a conversational style, *Integrated Business to Business Marketing* is both inclusive and engaging.

Mark Winter, President, Identity, Bingham Farms, MI 48025, US

Integrated Business To Business Marketing is one of the most comprehensive marketing books I have recently read. The author's understanding of marketing in places like Australia is impressive but the thing I like best about the book is that it offers a full turnkey solution without a ton of superfluous jargon which can simply confuse a reader who may have only limited marketing knowledge.

The book covers everything necessary to take a marketing campaign from zero to delivery, in an informal chatty style which is backed up with references to other successful businesses and personalities who have suffered the same hassles and pressures to successfully deliver, whether in the boardroom or even battlefield. This publication fills a gap in the marketplace for an informative B2B marketing book and it should be on the bookshelf of every marketing department.

Ken Aitken, Managing Director, SmartFreight part of Wisetech Global, Australia

Integrated Business To Business Marketing is a complete blueprint that can be followed by any aspiring business, to run an ongoing very successful marketing campaign. The book builds on the author's extensive knowledge of his subject and contains everything necessary to achieve sales on a long-term profitable basis. If you are only reading just one business book this year, this book is the one to read!

BJ Skrentny, Chairman, HMCA PLC, London and Yorkshire

This book should be on the reading list of every B2B marketeer, because it brings together different marketing activities which have often been treated in isolation. *Integrated Business To Business Marketing* is also very practical and clearly builds on the author's extensive knowledge and experience to provide a different perspective on B2B integrated marketing and how it should interface with sales. I found it to be written in a relaxed but informative style allowing the reader to easily absorb a lot of factual information. I particularly liked the highlighting of successful campaigns from a cross section of different countries and the check list at the end of each chapter to remind the reader of the key points.

Ann Harrison, Marketing Manager, HAE EHA, Solihull

Philip Allott draws together in one easily readable, accessible and logical book all the marketing fundamentals that every B2B business needs to know to survive and prosper. It is a comprehensive, well organised manual that should initially be read from cover to cover but then each topic can be accessed chapter by chapter as your plan develops.

It also explains in layman's terms some technical complexities that often perplex those who were educated prior to 1990!

Ian Fozard, Chairman Rooster's Brewery Ltd, North Yorkshire and Chairman of the Society of Independent Brewers

With his book *Integrated Business To Business Marketing*, the author, Philip Allott, has succeeded in creating an all-round hit in marketing and advertising for the B2B sector in the digital age. From multi-channel marketing to classic PR instruments and qualified lead generation, everything is included. It is thus aimed particularly at small and medium-sized companies. So these are well equipped for topics such as data analysis, SEO optimisation, cookies etc. Therefore, they can achieve the highest level of success with "marketing from a single source" - i.e. with a consistent appearance across all formats, channels and media. The cost aspect of marketing is not neglected either. In addition, easy-to-understand explanations, practical examples as well as concrete tips and checklists that can be implemented directly in the day-to-day running of the company can be found on all topics. The summaries at the end of each chapter ensure a lasting learning effect. This book should not be missing in any office of a B2B marketer.

Dr. Venera D'Elia, Head of Business Development, Möller Horcher Kommunikation, Germany

Integrated Business To Business Marketing is such an easy read, no jargon to try and understand, gives a very detailed but understanding of the market place, not only here but across many marketing countries. No matter what size of business, this is very insightful, very engaging and something I will share with my colleagues. A great step to step to be used across all businesses in a very well explained and easy format, you can't but grow your business.

Brenda Smith, Business Development Executive, Mondelez UK Limited

A useful and practical guide in how to develop your marketing strategy and plan for owners of all businesses, whatever the size, I particularly like the structure of the book which allows the reader to dip in and out of a particular topic, which is backed up with an action list summary at the end of each chapter.

Adrian Short, Director, Ulrick&Short Limited – Creators of clean and natural food ingredients for the food industry worldwide.

If you are looking for a buddy to get your business in flow and on track, *Integrated Business To Business Marketing: The Complete Blueprint* is the ideal companion for your B2B marketing journey.

It is a modern must-have checklist with a common sense approach ideal for fledgling and established businesses; Allott clearly describes the application of the most accessible, practical tools and processes in B2B marketing today.

The keen, common sense approach cuts through the noise of budgeting and decision making with business illustration.

Have it with you every step of the way ~ this go-to bible provides comprehensive structure for seasoned and student marketeers.

Adèle Winkley, Business & Alignment Consultant, Reiki Master, founder Concept to Creation, Pateley Bridge, England

Integrated Business To Business Marketing

The Complete Blueprint

Written specifically for business to
business marketing
Ideal for those with big ambitions but
limited time and budgets

Integrated Business To Business Marketing

The Complete Blueprint

Written specifically for business to
business marketing
Ideal for those with big ambitions but
limited time and budgets

Philip Allott

BUSINESS
BOOKS

Winchester, UK
Washington, USA

JOHN HUNT PUBLISHING

First published by Business Books, 2021
Business Books is an imprint of John Hunt Publishing Ltd., No. 3 East St., Alresford,
Hampshire SO24 9EE, UK
office@jhpbooks.com
www.johnhuntpublishing.com
www.johnhuntpublishing.com/business-books

For distributor details and how to order please visit the 'Ordering' section on our website.

ISBN: 978 1 78904 779 0
978 1 78904 780 6 (ebook)
Library of Congress Control Number: 2021936367

A CIP catalogue record for this book is available from the British Library.

Design: Stuart Davies

UK: Printed and bound by CPI Group (UK) Ltd, Croydon, CR0 4YY
Printed in North America by CPI GPS partners

We operate a distinctive and ethical publishing philosophy in
all areas of our business, from our global network of authors to
production and worldwide distribution.

Contents

With special thanks to my wife Sandra, my son Matthew, daughter Kirsty and my sister Kathy Cox and co-director Carol Rees who in the latter two cases painstakingly proof-read, cross referenced and adjusted every chapter where necessary. I would also like to thank my work colleagues John Abel, Rose Sims, Gary Allison, Evan Thomas and Oliver Heum for their proof-reading and/or support. Finally, a big thank you to my friend and business mentor Barney Skrentny (senior) for his words of encouragement.

Acknowledgements

The author would like to thank the following companies for their support and cooperation, Force24 Ltd, Selectabase Ltd, PRmax Ltd, SEMrush and last but certainly not least Allott and Associates Ltd.

Introduction

What is integrated marketing?

Whether your business is a start-up, family business and/or SME, large enterprise, part of a multinational conglomerate or PLC, the one thing it will always need is new and preferably more profitable sales. Understanding how to get good results without spending a king's ransom or burning the midnight oil to generate those sales is what this marketing book is about. Whether you are an established enterprise or start-up, *Integrated Business to Business Marketing* (AKA Integrated Marketing) has been written to provide a marketing blueprint.

In the history of the world there have never been so many different channels to communicate a marketing message. Email, Facebook, Twitter, LinkedIn, e-newsletters, direct mail, phone canvassing, websites and public relations may be the classic choices but what about permission marketing, advertising and emerging technologies like promotional cookies that can track visitors around the internet, and targeted social media advertising, digital publications with embedded QR (Quick Response) codes to trigger commentary from people featured and virtual exhibitions?

In an advanced digital era, with data available on almost everyone and everything, understanding how to bring these different technologies together and make it work to create new business sales is paramount to the success of any firm.

The aim of this book is to provide a practical, hands-on structured marketing blueprint, that the average aspiring or already successful reader can confidently use without needing to reinvent the wheel.

Without structured marketing which involves making the different promotional components work together rather than work in isolation and without a clear structure, the costs could be prohibitive and the actual deliverables most probably very disappointing.

If you're still not convinced, then let us look at the facts: there are around 5.9 million private sector businesses in the UK, BUT here is the killer statistic: almost 95% of them employ less than ten people,[1] 4.5 million have no employees and many provide a modest income for the business owner. The net rates of return of UK Private Non-financial Companies continues to fall.[2] Conversely, if a Company's productivity could increase by just 5%, this would add around $6,000 to the average annual wage packet and we'll return to this figure in Chapter 29. For now, it is worth noting that with limited staff resources, unless these firms are outsourcing their marketing or have introduced a structured and integrated marketing plan, then they will continue to remain small and possibly poorly performing.

However, wherever you are based there is no room for complacency. In the United States there are 28 million small businesses[3] but 22 million of these are small businesses with no other employees than the owner. In effect 75% of all US firms have no employees. In Canada there are only 1,167,978 businesses and 97.9% of these are SMEs, 54% of these firms employ four or less employees.[4] In Australia there are 2,375,753 actively trading businesses in the economy. However, 61% have no employees, 28% have 1 – 4 employees, 9% 5 – 19 employees and just 3% employ 20 or more personnel.[5] These figures are particularly important to bear in mind when purchasing data, and we'll come back to them and what they mean later in the book.

BUT if you want to be different - yes you - and increase your profit year on year, grow your business and really make things happen, then this book is for you. However, if you don't want to increase the profitability of your business, open up new markets and have the contracts you want rather than the work that

2

arrives, then I'd still urge you to read on because with proper integrated marketing your business could be so much better.

Running any business is a major challenge that is getting harder as each year passes. This is because successive governments have heaped regulation upon regulation onto firms, resulting in a plethora of rules and legally binding regulations.

Strict rules govern VAT payments, payroll, HR, premises, corporate taxation, mandatory staff pensions, planning, opening hours, data protection like GDPR (in the EU) and even what information can be legally stored on a work computer. To comply with these rules and many more, a whole training industry has been developed to provide courses to educate and cajole business owners into compliance. Government departments around the world send warning emails if a tax or duty payment has been missed and in Australia, they can even deduct it from your bank account. Accountants provide nudge guidance, information is published online and businesses, often with limited time resources for administration, and spend most of their spare capacity just trying to comply.

If this sounds all too familiar, you are not alone. Meeting these business regulations can be very time consuming, and who is doing the marketing and promoting the business, when you're distracted with admin tasks? The chances are: nobody!

As the least regulated industry (although this is changing thanks to data protection legislation) marketing is often the most misunderstood business activity and is often ignored, resulting in many companies simply marketing by default. From my experience few small medium enterprise (SME) companies fully understand the need for a proactive ongoing marketing campaign and, worse still, a number of the smaller firms often don't know where to start. Last year I met a business manager called Jim who said don't worry, I have next year's marketing all organised. What are you doing I asked? Oh it is going to be a great year, I have ordered 1,000 mugs and 500 calendars, so everything is sorted!

Sadly, there are still lots of Jims around and a few comparable male and female marketing managers who, through a lack of either training or experience, don't fully understand what marketing is about.

Let's be clear: marketing is about promoting products or services, hopefully supported with some prior market research.

The subsequent promotional tools may well encompass public relations, advertising, digital mailshots, website SEO (Search Engine Optimisation) and of course social media but doing any of these activities effectively is challenging. Just supposing you could achieve this by linking them all together and then measuring the results. The concept I have perfected brings all of these different marketing activities into one single cohesive force. The ultimate outcome is very effective integrated marketing or, in a nutshell, marketing utopia.

If this sounds too good to be true it isn't, because what I am going to show is the culmination of thirty years' experience. During the course of the next few chapters this book will demonstrate and provide your firm with the practical tools to turn a start-up business or 'steady as she goes' existing business into a high-performance marketing engine.

Come on, let's get started.

As you will see from the marketing wheel below the aim is to link all marketing actions together so they work together in sync and provide a higher return on investment.

A perfect starting point is a successful sale and the subsequent engagement of a customer to participate in a case study about the equipment or service your business has recently supplied. As part of the interview with the customer about the case study the interviewer should ask how many employees the firm has and the turnover of the business. Using SIC codes or

Allott's Integrated Market Wheel

an industry directory, this customer can also be matched with possibly another 50 – 500 companies with the same profile, using techniques outlined later in this book, for lead generation purposes.

The case study will talk about the improvements you have made to the customer's business; it must be written from the customer's perspective which after approval can be circulated to the trade media covering the sector that the customer trades with. This will also be read by your customer's competitors who are of course your future customers! Once publicity is created, links can be put on social media and media links to the story can be tweeted out on Twitter.

After a couple of weeks, the case study along with others can be edited and put into a digital newsletter, onto your website as news and used as testimonial snippets. The newsletter content should also hyperlink to your website to increase the dwell time of visitors. Meanwhile work should be under way to target the 50+ companies that match the profile of your customer and, after verifying them using the techniques outlined in subsequent pages, marketing can commence. Once contact and email details have been updated each contact should be sent a copy of the case study. This should be followed up within 24 hours by you or someone acting on your behalf by phone, this may require calls to each contact up to five times. Typically, this will generate 3–6 sales leads per 100 contacts. Welcome to the world of integrated marketing!

For the purposes of clarity, certain marketing actions have been grouped together. The aim is to allow the reader the opportunity to either follow the prescriptive process outlined or have the opportunity to skip to chapters of relevance.

1 Source the Federation of Small Businesses and Companies House
2 ONS Profitability of UK companies
3 https://www.chamberofcommerce.org/small-business-statistics/
4 www.ic.gc.ca/sbstatistics
5 Counts of Australian Businesses, including Entries and Exits, June 2015 to June 2019.

Chapter 1

Half of my marketing budget is wasted

Integrated marketing increases the reach of a business and allows more interaction with target customers. By increasing the number of marketing touches to each contact, it increases the chances of a potential customer becoming an actual customer.

US department store owner John Wanamaker is attributed with saying "half my marketing budget is wasted but I don't know which half." The same mantra was later taken up by Henry Ford. However, despite this costly problem, Wanamaker and subsequently Ford still needed to market if they were to realise their respective businesses' full sales potential.

Many firms continue to face the same dilemma because countless businesses, even some large ones, don't always put in place the systems to measure outcomes or to be more precise something that will measure the return on their investment (ROI) - see chapter 26 for more details.

Marketing is also one of the least mechanised business functions often resulting in massive duplication and sometimes triplication of key activities. This lack of coordination can often spill over into the sales effort. In some key business to business (B2B) sectors, sales often rely on the perceived efforts of one super sales person, who may even be the business owner, possibly supported by a cabal of marginally performing sales colleagues.

However, just supposing that rather than depending on a single sales person your business could utilise a suite of integrated, coordinated marketing activities that generate business leads month after month, and provide sufficient sales to turn a marginally performing business into increased profits and if applicable turn its sales team into high achievers.

Welcome to integrated marketing.

Great sales don't usually just happen, they require good market research, great planning and subsequently fantastic execution.

The idea of integrated marketing is to harness past sales to leverage further successful sales. However, if you are launching a new business you will still need to try and define your relevant target market. A good starting point is to look at your competitors and examine any case studies on their website. This will provide a useful steer and allow data to be purchased from a reputable list broker that matches the target sector. Data can be purchased by industry sector, geography, turnover, employee numbers and even profitability – the latter is very useful because it stops you chasing work from lossmaking companies. I'll explain this in far more detail in chapters three and four.

Let me first of all explain the concept in further detail. Just supposing for the purpose of explanation that you are selling machinery or a service like insurance and have recently got a profitable order or policy from a food manufacturer. To identify other potential food companies who may also benefit from your services you should initially research your current food customer by asking the buying contact how many employees it has and the firm's turnover. Even if the contact is only partly or even not at all cooperative, some of the information, depending on the size of the business, may also be available in the public domain, such as UK's Companies House, in the US and Canada the Federal authorities or in Australia the ASIC and New Zealand the Securities & Investment Commission. Please see chapter three for more information and also about using list brokers.

Assuming the company has 30 employees and an estimated turnover of $10 million, I would recommend that a search is made for companies with 25 – 50 employees and an estimated turnover of between $5 million and $15 million. The most important thing is not to target every food firm but to break the project down into manageable data chunks.

Calling 50 companies is relatively straightforward, calling 1,500 where many are small and don't have a budget even if they decide to buy hardware, is a nightmare.

Presupposing a formal search indicates that there are around 100 companies with between 25 and 50 employees. You should order this data (we'll talk about data providers later), which will most likely come with just the managing director's name. Therefore, subsequent phone research will be needed to identify the person at each company who buys the relevant machinery or service like insurance. Depending on the firm it is most likely to be the production manager or chief engineer.

The key task is to phone each firm and get the name of the person responsible, their job title and email address and if available their mobile phone and direct dial number. Most receptionists will provide this information although will be less keen to let you speak to the relevant contact, which at this stage is irrelevant anyway. Complete the research and record everything into a spreadsheet or CMS (contact management software) and then move on. (We'll also talk about databases in a subsequent chapter.)

If you hit a large number of no names due to company policy - this is especially likely in the pharmaceutical sector - try and work out each company's email policy eg., first.surname@ which is most likely an email domain name that matches the website address of the company. Please be mindful that in some countries there are limitations on data processing unless the name is in the public domain via a public records office like Companies House or social media where the individual has chosen to identify themselves.

The latter allows a search of LinkedIn using the company's name to see who is associated with the company. It may be that from identifying a key contact such as a managing director you can see who they are linked with and whether an individual's job description matches the job title of the person you need to contact who will subsequently be referred to as the sales prospect. It is ironic that company directors spend a fortune restricting access through reception screening procedures but are happy to puff out their chests on LinkedIn and talk in detail about their specific responsibilities.

Once you have appropriate contacts, email (or write) to each of the identified sales prospects with a personalised email or letter and if possible, with a flyer outlining your product or service.

Follow-up the correspondence with a phone call within 24 hours and try each sales prospect with five attempts, but do remember that more senior people are busy and therefore whilst they may be interested in your product or service, they won't normally return your calls. From personal experience this should generate a core of around six sales leads per 100 contacts for subsequent further discussions and possibility of a sales visit and/or quotation.

The remaining ninety-odd companies are all still relevant (remember you have already researched these for accuracy), it is just that they don't have a suitable project or are already entrenched with one of your competitors. These ninety-odd names should be kept warm by circulating them quarterly information such as an e-newsletter.

Ask the original food customer that placed an order with you if you can give them some free publicity. Most medium ranking companies are always up for free publicity providing it is positive and reinforces their brand.

If your company hasn't yet achieved a sale to allow a case study to be written, but would like to promote its capability to the food sector, consider doing a press release concerning the targeting of the industry and what your equipment or service can do to improve the food industry.

The case study or press release will need writing in a

reasonably professional way, with a small number of hyperlinks back to your website, which will be explained in chapter 13. For now, assume that you have shown the draft to the food firm and after a few changes they have approved it. Following approval circulate the release to the food and beverage trade media. There are around 100 relevant UK publications, fewer in the US, Canada and individual EU countries.[1]

Once the publicity has started to appear in some of the digital titles, create a social media hyperlink to the relevant magazine text and promote the link via Twitter, Facebook and LinkedIn. Also remember to have the social media channels linked to your website because this helps with search engine optimisation and will improve your Google ranking.

The original press release or case study can now be used as content for an e-newsletter and even an advert or advertorial. After 30 days the press release or case study can also be added to your website as news content and the case studies as successful examples of your work. Whilst this all might sound straightforward, the truth is that many SMEs don't properly market because they lack structure, their marketing employees' cherry pick tasks and/or they don't grasp the importance of integrated marketing.

A little amending for the e-newsletter should suffice and this can then be sent to prospective customers known to your business and the ninety-odd companies researched earlier as part of the telemarketing campaign.

Hopefully you will have noticed on this marketing journey how all the activities so far interface with each other. Welcome to integrated marketing.

Key points and actions you need to take from this chapter

1 - Try and understand the concept of integrated marketing
2 - It is likely that only 5 or 10% of the potential customers

are relevant, the rest are likely to have a turnover that is too small

3   - To approach these potential customers it needs a rifle rather than a machine gun approach

4   - Integrated marketing maintains a dialogue after you stop speaking to the customer

1   Source PRmax

Chapter 2

Initial campaign planning and why many campaigns fail

Planning and running a good integrated marketing campaign requires research, refinement, patience and an element of luck. However, the more research and planning you do the less luck you need.

If you are a golfer you may remember the adage 'The Harder I Practice, the Luckier I Get' and so it is with marketing although in this case your practice is the pre-prep homework you do before starting the campaign and your post-game is the post evaluation of your marketing campaign. The starting point for any marketing is to determine (from some initial customer research) who you want to reach and what you want to say. Don't worry too much about the actual marketing vehicles you want to reach the targets with, as at this stage all that is needed is to define the target audience and messages. We'll come onto strategy, messages, tactics and marketing channels later.

Just determining your target audience can take up to a few days and if you think that's long, just think of the military. During the Second World War, the invasion of Europe from the UK involved months of work just to determine the best places to launch the invasion (reach the target audience). Planning staff were appointed in March 1943, but the detailed work to follow up didn't get going until January 1944.

Your research to agree the targets should involve identifying the following:

- Target customers
- Position of the target contact with the target customer i.e., managing director, production manager, accountant, HR

etc
- Turnover bands of companies
- Number of employees
- Geographical restrictions
- Sector the target company operates within
- The estimated size of the market for your product or service
- Other nice to know information such as the number of years established and their profitability

As a starting point you must look at existing customers, or if you are a start-up business the potential customers you would like to trade with.

Many marketing campaigns fail because marketeers are too optimistic or blinded to the fact that there is not an infinite number of businesses to target. Let's take a recent really topical subject. Supposing you sell standalone oxygen generators like Oxair in Australia and want to reach medical ventilator manufacturers worldwide to offer them a total solution.

If you believed the news you might be fooled into believing there are hundreds of thousands of ventilator manufacturers. The reality is something totally different.

Just over 50% of the worldwide market share is held by just five companies: Philips Healthcare (Netherlands), ResMed Inc. (US), Medtronic plc (Ireland), Becton, Dickinson and Company (US), and Getinge Group (Sweden).

The bigger remaining players in this market are Dräger Group (Germany), Smiths Group plc (UK), Teleflex Incorporated (US), Hamilton Medical AG (Switzerland), and GE Healthcare (US) Fisher & Paykel (New Zealand), Air Liquide (France), Zoll Medical (US), Allied Healthcare Products (US), Airon Mindray (China), and Schiller (Switzerland).[1]

Sorry to get to a company naming level but I wish to strongly make an important point: no matter how you aggregate the data, taking into account the total number of players there are only a limited number of companies to reach and therefore you may need to reconsider your campaign by thinking outside the box and, in this case, targeting the actual hospitals because these hospitals will already have ventilators but may be using bottled oxygen. This creates a converse problem because with too much data you may need to segment your integrated marketing into a country by country or even county by county or state by state programme of delivery.

The alternative approach if you are intent on just reaching the ventilator makers is to have a very interventionist combined marketing and sales campaign. This is because no matter how you configure the ventilator data there are not enough manufacturers to justify a fully integrated marketing campaign and therefore the campaign is likely to fail without a high level of sales intervention through phone calls and potential visits.

Remapping out your campaign to reach hospitals who are the ultimate users of most ventilators will put your campaign into a very different mode. In the OECD there are over 2 million acute beds and 73,585 critical care beds,[2] most needing an oxygen feed.

Okay so where do you source this initial marketing data? Well the next chapter provides detailed information on suppliers and different options. However, at this stage you need to learn as much as possible about your target markets. Depending on what and who you are targeting it might also be possible to buy an off the shelf ready-made report, suppliers include: www.store.mintel.com, www.reportsinsights.com, www.grandviewresearch.com, www.researchandmarkets.com and www.ibisworld.com

I have used Ibisworld, which has a lot of manufacturing reports, in the past and found the quality of the report very good which enabled me to finish a marketing report to a high standard. However, just a word of caution - some of these reports can be very broad and also dated, so always read what is in the contents report before purchasing.

If you are still unsure, download the free sample report many of the suppliers offer to see if it covers the level of detail you need.

Your business may be a member of a trade association, if so ask your membership contact whether they already get the report and if so can you read it, before you purchase a copy!

Another source of useful information is the annual reports many of the larger companies provide within their annual accounts. This might include market share information, subsidiaries trading under another name that could be targeted and basic information such as profitability and future investment plans.

The more initial research you can do to determine the viability of your campaign, the greater the likely success. However, do not be afraid to think outside the box and also remember the sales rewards that will eventually flow when you get it right.

Campaigns often fail because people don't learn from their mistakes. Remember you have not got a god given right to succeed or for that matter fail. There are a number of companies that have had decades of bad luck but through continual marketing and technical innovation have turned the corner and become the best in the world.

As a shining example, Apple is currently one of the world's most successful businesses. One of the reasons for its success is a dynamic, constantly developing business plan, which its founder Steve Jobs created after intently studying the market to understand the heartbeat of its target audience.

Apple started its life as just another computer company like many others, but most of those rivals have dramatically disappeared. Can many remember the ZX Spectrum, Commodore 64 or even the Amstrad PCW 8256? What gets lost in this equation is that Apple has not always been the kind of world-beating success it is today. Can anyone remember the Pippin, G4 Cube or Apple Newton of which the latter although a failure, was a forerunner to the iPhone? What Steve Jobs did for Apple was to take these product failures, continually refine its marketing messages and products by learning valuable lessons from failure.

At my own office we have a notice that says: "Be aware of those two great imposters success and failure."

The truth is that all greatest entrepreneurs know about failure: Henry Ford filed for bankruptcy twice before eventually succeeding with the Ford Motor Company. As Jeff Bezos told Amazon shareholders in a letter: "Failure comes part and parcel with invention. It's not optional. We understand that and believe in failing early and iterating until we get it right."

Don't be afraid to innovate with your marketing and if it doesn't work out the first time, treat it as a learning exercise and evaluate what went wrong and then start again. The money you invested may have been even less than going on a training course but just think what you have learned! If you are innovating and are concerned there is a high risk start your marketing as a pilot and then ramp it up. The key thing is to do something - as English humourist, satirist, and author Terry Pratchett said: "The worst thing you can do is nothing."

Key points and actions you need to take from this chapter

1 - Determine your audience and do some initial research
2 - Do a reality check that there are sufficient companies to target, if not look at allied markets where there are significantly more businesses or organisations to target
3 - See your campaign as a starting point and don't be afraid if at first you don't succeed
4 - Learn from your mistakes and keep innovating your marketing until you get it right

5   - If you are unsure run a pilot and then ramp up the campaign

6   - Don't forget those two great imposters "success and failure"

1   RnR Market Research

2   https://en.wikipedia.org/wiki/List_of_countries_by_ hospital_beds

Chapter 3

Understanding B2B data, sloppy data kills sales

Understanding B2B data is at the core of integrated marketing, because sloppy data will stop your marketing from even starting, which is why all data must be verified.

According to science fiction author Bruce Sterling, the level of ignorance is declining and the ability to accumulate data and manipulate it for various ends is increasing.

Despite having access to marketing data it doesn't necessarily mean that a business always knows how to interrogate it. Take the example of my neighbour Chris, he runs a small part time picture painting business from home which for tax efficiency reasons he decided to list as a small limited company. In the UK portable appliance testing (PAT) is a very competitive market and within a few weeks of establishing his business my neighbour started getting repeat calls from a PAT firm. Despite his protests that he is a one-man, small business Chris got ten unwanted phone calls and in the end was driven to formally complain to the MD of the PAT firm to get the calls stopped. The PAT outfit must have wasted hours of resources on my neighbour, all because they had bought a list of new businesses in the local area that they service but then failed to do some very basic verification work to determine the actual size of those business before launching into a so-called targeted campaign.

Targeting the wrong sized companies is like pouring marketing resources down the drain. Even worse it ties up a sales force on benign calls when they could be talking to a sales lead with true potential.

I have called this chapter sloppy data kills sales, but it should really be called getting good quality data that can be managed creates sales. This is because despite the likely howls from database suppliers concerning the accuracy of their information, it is only as good as the data the suppliers can access and research.

There are still only a small number of primary sources for business data. Most of the list providers use information from one or more of the following sources:

The Government via Companies House or Federal
    Authorities
Telephone validating and data collecting companies such as
    Thomson Local and 118
Local authority information like licensing, economic
    development, planning and rating
Trade associations and professional membership
    organisations
Exhibition guides
Specialist sector list compliance firms
Online phone directories such as Yell.com
Free business listing sites

In the UK, the US and Australia most advanced economies database compliers rely on the basic content from Companies House or its equivalent. This is because by law all limited companies are required to do a statutory declaration each year, providing basic information such as the names of its directors, a registered address and some financial information.

Incorporated companies have a limited time to file their annual accounts, typically within nine months of the financial year end. In the UK, US, Canada and Australia there are also other statutory legal accounting obligations that companies have to meet.

A lot can happen in nine months and if the database provider is relying on a company's annual financial statement for their core data without researching it further then it may be very inaccurate.

Old in-house databases should be ignored, in effect anything twelve months or older is starting to become obsolete and should be discarded or, resource permitting, revalidated by telephone.

Also remember if you are based in places like the UK, EU and California, there is strict data protection legislation in place that requires your business to demonstrate things like legitimate interests in the event of complaints. Trying to justify this when using very old data puts you on the back foot before you even defend your case.

However, don't despair, because buying data is the start of your campaign not the end of it and with further work you should have more accurate data and consequently some great marketing results In fact I am so confident I am staking my reputation on it.

In the UK reputable list brokers such as Selectabase, Kompass and Thomson Local Direct Marketing Services may use various sources of data, which could include Companies House and business directory information.

Likewise, in the US and Canada list providers such as Kompass, Harvest Business Lists, InfoDepots, D&B Hoovers (a subsidiary of Dun & Bradstreet), Lead411 and Cornerstone also use basic public data from the federal government and additional information provided by phone companies.

Data provided by many suppliers for middle ranking companies is often limited, sometimes historical, but mostly accurate in the context of the core information such as address details; some of the providers even give an accuracy guarantee. However, for many businesses it will not provide relevant contact details such as the production manager's name or their email address.

It is also worth noting that some bigger providers also pool and rebadge data, which can lead to marketplace confusion.

A good quality database in an easily manipulated (usable) format is one of the most important pillars of a good marketing campaign.

I recently met a multinational machinery food manufacturing firm, which has bases in 50 different countries around the world including the US, Australia, Canada and the UK. The business has a state-of-the-art customer relationship management (CRM) database that records everything, which it launched in 2016. However, despite a substantial marketing budget the company had no cohesive database strategy and the sales team was permitted to import obsolete contact data dating back many years. A swift examination of the database quickly identified some companies that had ceased trading, contacts that had retired and three different trading name entries for a company that had changed names three times in just a few years. In effect despite the investment in an expensive CRM, much of the data imported was useless!

The issue is not always about the quality of the data, although this is obviously important, but the lack of relevance. For example, supposing your company is selling stationery, emailing the managing director of a 200-employee business using a generic email address such as enquiries@joebloggs.com is a pointless exercise. Understanding basic data, no matter how boring, is the key to the success of your marketing campaign.

In the UK as of July 2019, there were around 3.5 million people self-employed, 4.2 million limited companies[1] and 405,000 partnerships in the UK, BUT a massive 95% of these businesses were micro-businesses who employ 0-9 people. Only 41% of the firms are even registered for VAT and/or PAYE.

In the US there are 28 million businesses but again here is the killer statistic: 22 million of these firms are self-employed with no payroll staff.[2] In effect 75% of all US firms have no employees. In Canada there are only 1,167,978 businesses and 97.9% of these are SMEs, 54% of these firms employ four or less employees.[3] In Australia there are 2,121,235 businesses however 61% have no employees, 28% have 1–4 employees, 9% 5–19 employees and just 3% employ 20 or more personnel.[4]

In the UK service industries account for 74% of businesses, 79% of employment and 71% of turnover. The manufacturing sector accounts for 5% of businesses, 10% of employment and 16% of turnover.

It is vital that you grasp the importance of business size because B2B marketing is all about reaching the firms you need to speak with and not wasting valuable marketing resources on the wrong sized companies. No matter how good the supplier of your data may claim to be, if it doesn't come with employee numbers and turnover, don't buy it!

The majority of UK non-limited firms are small and with no independent annual statutory information the business owners are free if they are inclined, to make up information if they are contacted by a researcher. Depending on your product or service these companies may or may not be relevant. For example, if your business is selling professional indemnity insurance, they are very relevant, however trying to promote a new multimillion-pound or dollar corporate headquarters to firms which are still based at the founder's home would be a massive waste of marketing resources.

Every year substantial sums of money are wasted by marketing departments buying the names from a list broker of every company in a particular sector. These marketing departments subsequently discover that most of the target firms are too small to service, but often only after devoting a telemarketing team to hours of fruitless calling and/or sending out countless digital mailing material and video links. Don't make this common mistake, define your target size companies before buying the data.

Choosing data and then researching it further is critical to the success or failure of a campaign. Most data will be supplied by a list broker with a default contact such as a managing director's name. However, it is likely that you may need a different contact such as the production manager.

As a golden rule never assume that sending something to the managing director will reach the production manager and never assume if it did, that the production manager will take any notice of the managing director.

To determine the data required you need to build a profile around your company's most successful sales. At a first glance these existing customers may not have much in common with each other, however drill down a bit further at turnover, industry subsector, employee numbers, products, geography, common trade publications and even culture and you should see some kind of correlation.

If you are a start-up business you will need to attempt to define the market for your products or service and then try and visualise the likely recipients and beneficiaries. Write down on a single sheet of paper the type of potential users and their geographical location. What size of company turnover would benefit most, are there any types of companies apart from competitors that should be ignored?

A good starting point is to take a look at your biggest competitors. Do they have customer case studies that are in the public domain or website downloadable? Or a website list of customers or other useful information that you can use to help calculate the size of companies you should be targeting? If so, you can now work out the type of data you need.

Key points and actions you need to take from this chapter

1 - Understand how data is accumulated, there are no silver bullets

2 - The majority of companies in the advanced world are extremely small and are unlikely to provide a profitable

return for the marketing investment to reach them

3   - Accurate data is more important than volume

4   - Understand the local rules around making contact and try and work with them

5   - Determine the type of data you need by researching existing customers and by looking at the type of customers your competitors are attracting

1   Companies House data published July 2019 https://www. gov.uk/government/news/uk-company-statistics-2018- to-2019

2   www.forbes.com/sites/jasonnazar/2013/09/09/16-surprising- statistics-about-small-businesses/2/#49e59335585d

3   www.ic.gc.ca/sbstatistics

4   Counts of Australian Businesses, including Entries and Exits, Jun 2011 to Jun 2015

Chapter 4

Making B2B data generate new sales

Targeting the right size of potential customers is key to the success of integrated marketing, and understanding who they are will enable your marketing campaign to flourish.

Let us assume that you have decided, based on your earlier target customer profiling, that you wish to target companies employing between 25 and 50 people and with an assumed turnover of between $5 million and $10 million comprising all companies in the food production sector (food breaks down into more than 25 subsections and that is excluding any beverages). Let's also assume you want to reach the production manager at each firm.

The next step is to determine what numbers are available for contacting. Depending on workable numbers some compromise may be needed to get the right figures but at this stage let's do the data search. Remember B2B integrated marketing works best in batches of 100 names.

A number of the database providers allow searches to be completed online without any commitment to purchase. This is really helpful because it allows the marketer to model the data using a few searches before buying.

Everyone will develop a favourite database supplier, for the UK market I prefer Selectabase because you can buy as you need online without the need to commit to a minimum order quantity. If you are reading this book and based elsewhere in the world try Kompass, which is represented in most large countries or Harvest Business Contacts for the US, Canada and Australia. The information provided from both companies is comprehensive. Kompass has business data for 66 countries representing 4,991,219 companies and 16,732,975 contacts.

However, remember it is the quality of the data that matters and the flexibility of the database supplier, not the volume.

Selectabase works in a similar format to most online data sources but like all software you need to become familiar with it to understand the different field options and how the data download section of its website operates to achieve the most benefits. The Selectabase team are just a phone call away and can offer honest and impartial advice to help you get the right lists. Selectabase allows data to be selected by exact postcode, county or radius of a particular postcode, perhaps centred around your office which is really helpful for targeting serviceable areas. For the purposes of this fictional campaign to target food companies, I have left the Selectabase default settings as UK wide.

The default settings for telephone numbers is "Telephone numbers where available", and "Remove numbers unsafe for marketing calls." This is important if you intend to call these firms. In the UK both businesses and individuals have the right to register for FREE to specify if they wish to receive cold calls. Those who register on the TPS /CTPS register should not be contacted by telephone. The Corporate Telephone Preference Service (CTPS) is a central opt out register whereby corporate subscribers can register their wish not to receive unsolicited sales and marketing telephone calls, to either all of their organisation's telephone numbers, or to certain numbers.

It is a legal requirement in the UK that companies do not make such calls to numbers registered on the CTPS. Therefore, companies listed as TPS or CTPS should not be cold called unless you already have an existing relationship as, say, a past supplier or through social media contact like LinkedIn.

This is a real bind and some marketing companies go to great lengths to try and establish a relationship by giving away freebies and using other permission marketing techniques, consequently I have devoted a whole chapter to discuss this in more detail later in the book.

Most database suppliers have various job titles and email options but because these contacts (excluding TPS) are going to be independently researched by me or you, I have left the Specific Contacts/Job Function settings as: any.

There are options to select by SIC, NAICS or just Industry Sector.

SIC (Standard Industry Classification) codes originated in the US in 1937 to provide a unified approach to data management and are based on a four-digit code. SIC codes are organised into increasingly wider industry classifications: industry group, major group, and division. The first three digits of the SIC code indicate the industry group, and the first two digits indicate the major group. Each division encompasses a range of SIC codes. Over time the codes have been adopted by Governments around the world and are currently used in the UK by Companies House. In 1997 the US moved to the North American Industry Classification System (NAICS code) which is more accurate because it is based on a six-digit code, although confusingly some parts of the Federal Government like the US Securities and Exchange are still using SIC codes.

As an example, SIC code 2024 (which comprises ice cream and frozen desserts) fits to industry group 202 (comprising dairy products), which is part of major group 20 (food and kindred products), which in turn belongs to the division of manufacturing.

Confusingly, different database providers are offering either SIC, NAICS or both plus their own in-house classifications.

From my own experience some database suppliers provide more data by sector if you use their own industry sectors such as food, although this may not be broken down into as many sub segments between the different sectors. It should be noted that this does vary between database providers and if you are using Kompass in the US, Australia, Canada or elsewhere I would recommend that you adopt their own industry classifications, because these are generally far more comprehensive than using a SIC code.

As a test try searching by SIC and then a broad sector such as food. In most cases food will provide more names than SIC search although in the case of food it may include a few divisions such as beverages or fats which you may not wish to target. For the purposes of our fictional food campaign it should also be remembered that with many database suppliers, food companies can also appear in a number of sub categories, in this instance reflecting the food industry's close links to farming. Therefore a common-sense judgement call is needed. For example, the sub category 'production of meat and poultry meat products' may or may not be relevant to your product or service as some company functions such as packaging may be completed offsite. Ultimately this may only be determined from a telephone validation conversation so at this stage these database prospects should be included.

For this example, I have selected the UK SIC 2007 code and have chosen all relevant food listings which are likely to include arcane terms like 'Manufacture of oils and fats.' Remember food is just for illustration purposes and your search terms are likely to be very different, although the principle of searching remains the same:

- Processing and preserving of meat
- Processing and preserving of poultry meat
- Production of meat and poultry meat products
- Processing and preserving of fish, crustaceans and molluscs
- Processing and preserving of potatoes
- Manufacture of fruit and vegetable juice
- Other processing and preserving of fruit and vegetables
- Manufacture of oils and fats
- Manufacture of margarine and similar edible fats

- Operation of dairies and cheese making
- Liquid milk and cream production
- Butter and cheese production
- Manufacture of milk products (other than liquid milk and cream, butter, cheese)
- Manufacture of ice cream
- Manufacture of breakfast cereals and cereals-based foods
- Manufacture of bread; manufacture of fresh pastry goods and cakes
- Manufacture of rusks and biscuits; manufacture of preserved pastry goods and cakes
- Manufacture of macaroni, noodles, couscous and similar farinaceous products
- Manufacture of sugar
- Manufacture of cocoa and chocolate confectionery
- Manufacture of sugar confectionery
- Tea processing
- Production of coffee and coffee substitutes
- Manufacture of condiments and seasonings
- Manufacture of prepared meals and dishes
- Manufacture of homogenised food preparations and dietetic food
- Manufacture of other food products

As you will see many of the search terms sound a bit arcane because as already explained some of the categories date back to the 1930s. Work through the list ticking all relevant boxes until you have exhausted the list.

If you are using Selectabase, leave "ADVANCED - No. of Employees (at Site or Business)" as the default setting ("Employees At Site") and move on to selecting number of employees (Actual or Estimated). Set at more than 25 and less than 51. The precise settings will vary between different database providers. However, don't worry providing it roughly correlates. At this lower level of employee numbers always use estimated because it will again provide more information.

Finally, add the turnover parameters we mentioned earlier in this chapter - between $5 million and $10 million.

The final total at the time of writing is 118 companies (excludes any CTPS firms) that meet the criteria and are worth prospecting.

If the turnover flags are removed the search increases to 363 companies and if the number of employees is changed to any, the number of food companies increases to 7,083 records.

The majority of the 7,083 companies are small and therefore even if they were interested in buying machinery or an expensive service it is questionable whether the firms would have the capital to purchase.

I can't emphasise enough, be selective with the companies you target, go for the Goldilocks solution based on just the right size and then put the maximum effort into chasing these firms. If you target massive corporations you may hit a solid brick wall and if you go for small, you may find a soft and friendly business but one with a no budget brick wall.

Let's go with the 118 contacts and download them from the vendor in a spreadsheet format.

Just to reiterate this is the start of the process and having bought the data you will need to find out who the decision-making contact is for the product or service you wish to sell.

There are times when no matter how hard you try none of the database suppliers can provide the data needed. I had a recent experience of this when one of my clients wanted an e-cigarette database, which at the time was such a new industry no such comprehensive database exists. To meet the challenge, online data was researched using Yell.com as the initial starting point. The e-cigarette companies were subsequently each phoned to identify the person responsible for buying new equipment and their direct email address.

Permission was also sought to send each of them an email with an attached leaflet. In the UK 120 companies were identified of which around 50 manufactured e-liquids.

The subsequent phone follow-up of the e-cigarette companies generated ten sales leads of which three went on to order labelling and packaging equipment, which in turn paid for the campaign many times over. Just because a conventional database doesn't exist it doesn't mean that there is not a need for your product or service. Conversely, because a database didn't exist the rookie competitors weren't able to reach the e-cigarette market. This resulted in far more of those contacted by phone being willing to engage in the sales process.

The data, whether purchased from a list broker or from your own research, needs putting into some kind of prospective customer relationship management system (CRM). Depending on the size of your business it may be that you already have an in-house system or need to purchase a solution.

If you are looking for a software database solution there are a number of options available. The first is to have a CRM specially written, although this is likely to be time consuming and expensive, the latter making it a challenge for many smaller firms.

The alternative is to purchase one of the standard packages. There are a number of providers including GoldMine, Salesforce, ACT! and BASE. Some of the systems like Salesforce and BASE are designed to be cloud based with the advantage that your sales team can access information on the move but with the downside that a monthly fee in perpetuity is required.

GoldMine, which has been around much longer, is popular with salespeople and companies however it is not always intuitive to use.

My own preference is ACT! because of the flexibility it offers and I know it can do everything expounded in this book as I use ACT! almost every working day.

Whether you are using an existing CRM or plan to purchase a system please ensure you spend sufficient time pre-planning to ensure there are appropriate fields and categories allocated to the database to help you distinguish between data imported now and future data imports.

From past experience it is quite common for junior members of staff to import new data into the same database fields as existing data without any way of subsequently identifying the new data, simply because the marketing department has not taken the time and care to define how they would like the database managing.

Remember marketing data should be treated with the same respect as financial data. After all you wouldn't import last month's financial accounts into this month's financial accounts without separately labelling them as say September 2020 and October 2020, so please do practice the same convention with marketing data.

All database packages come with fields for entering the contact, email address, postal address, phone and cell phone details. However, additional bespoke fields should be allocated for when the data was imported, source of data, employee numbers, turnover (if available) and sector of activity.

ACT! allows its spare user fields to be renamed and data can also be segregated into groups. This allows hot prospects, different emailing campaigns and sectors to be put into a particular or, if applicable, multiple groups. The use of groups allows 100 records to be immediately looked up on screen from a total database that could comprise 25,000 records!

Particular attention should be spent on ensuring that email addresses are correctly imported. Because all of the packages mentioned allow multiple email marketing, we'll discuss this in more detail in the next two chapters.

Identifying the target customers, importing the data and putting it into the right categories is just the start of the process.

The next challenge is to identify the right person you need to contact, which for the purposes of our fictional campaign we have called the production manager.

This is possibly the most important part of the process. It is so important that I have devoted later in this book a whole chapter to telemarketing and how to navigate past challenging receptionists. However, in this early section of integrated marketing you don't need any particular skills other than the resolution to phone each of the contacts and ask the receptionist the name of the person who would decide whether to buy your product or service.

Once you have a name ask for their email address, job title and extension number. Most firms will provide the majority of this information. If they stall on giving you an email address try and work it out using the firm's website domain name and whether email addresses are philip.allott@, philip@ or philipallott@ or pallott@

There are also sites like Hunter (https://hunter.io) which enable you to test email addresses.

A good way of finding out the email sequence with a receptionist is to ask for their email address, most will volunteer an address as a way of protecting the more senior people.

If you are still unsure about the email address Google your contact's name and email, some bigger companies even list key employees' email addresses on their website.

Where applicable carefully insert the updated contact information into your CRM which should replace the existing name and any generic email address. Once this phase has been correctly completed, you should congratulate yourself because you have defined the direction of your integrated marketing and done part of the hardest part of any campaign, some of the strategy. In the coming chapters I will show how to put a campaign together behind your newly verified database.

Key points and actions you need to take from this chapter

1 - No matter how good the supplier of your data may claim to be if it doesn't come with employee and turnover figures, don't buy it!

2 - Ask your supplier for some sample data because most of the suppliers expect you to pay cash with order, which provides little recourse if you get it wrong

3 - Profile your existing (best customers) and find out, if possible, their SIC, NAICS or business sector. This needs to include turnover, sector, geography and the number of employees

4 - Manage your data through a CRM, make sure you have categories to record everything and that you and your team use it properly

5 - Getting data is the start of the process not the end, for accuracy you'll need to identify the right contact for your goods or services and their contact details for each company

Chapter 5

Digital Marketing: why, how and to who – why targeting your campaign to specific audiences is so important

To get the best from any digital campaign it must be part of integrated marketing and, in addition, it should be noted that due to the niche nature of many B2B markets there is a limited number of targets. Therefore a consumer machine gun type approach trying to reach as many people as possible just won't work.

Every business, even if it has just one employee which might even be you, needs to expand and digital marketing subject to certain caveats is one of the methods to achieve this. Due to a wealth of different options and service providers, getting started with email marketing which forms the backbone of digital marketing is no longer as difficult or challenging as it was just a few years ago. Digital marketing also provides many more options to create dynamic, interactive content to communicate often dull information in a more interesting format.

Email marketing a few years ago was seen as an easy marketing fix for generating sales leads, but today this is no longer the case and much greater attention must be paid to which recipients should be targeted. The use of email marketing falls broadly into two camps: finding new customers and staying in touch with existing customers and those where some kind of contact has already been established but where no purchase transaction has yet been forthcoming.

Email marketing is used in a number of different ways and a brief description of the main purposes is listed below, although it should be noted that there are endless variations.

E-marketing letter – preferably opening the door to a subsequent telephone follow-up

E-blasts – normally a one-page template promoting a single offer or service

E-newsletter – sent to prospective and existing customers to inform them of products or services. This is great for promoting offers and also keeping in contact with likely sales prospects

Digital storyboards – this allows the opportunity to send the prospective customer on a journey using a series of digital storyboards comprising text and graphics. These can be set up through platforms like Force24 to be automated and if the customer doesn't respond to the first message, a second message, third and fourth can be sent after a certain set interval. This method is particularly popular at the moment because it can act as part of the seven touches typically needed before a prospective customer engages

Most consumer suppliers and a growing proportion of B2B suppliers are increasingly using e-newsletters as a means of staying in touch with their core (target) post and pre-sale customer base. This has the advantage of reducing the need for as many phone calls, provides a quick and readily accessible outlet for special offers and reminding prospects (who possibly receive up to 200 emails or more a day) that you exist.

As part of an integrated marketing approach, your campaign is invested in all four types of email marketing but as a starting point we'll be initially talking about e-marketing letters because this is where your campaign will start.

There are a number of ways of circulating email material, one of which could be direct from your CRM system which interfaces with Microsoft 365.

Using this method to reach B2B prospects creates limitations on the type of design that can be used. This is because Microsoft Outlook places certain restrictions on the email template design.

Unfortunately, Microsoft Outlook remains the dominant business email package still used by the majority of business recipients.

If you want to see companies that have exceeded the design spec, just look at the number of email newsletters that initially arrive as a series of x marking the spot where the picture still needs to be downloaded or, worse for the supplier, those that go straight into your spam box.

As a guide if the email exceeds 100KB in size or fails the spam ping test or has too many images inserted at the start, the chances are that your emailer will go into the spam filter or possibly even get deleted before it reaches the target's email inbox.

Microsoft Office 365 also places restrictions on the amount of outgoing emails that can be sent: normally a maximum of 150 emails can be sent out although fewer if there are attachments. After 150 emails Office 365 will lock the account and won't allow any further emails to be circulated until the account is reset at portal level, which is a pain.

There are also some legal restrictions in the UK, US, Canada and most other first world countries, which restrict what is possible. One firm highlights on its website a few simple and sensible rules to comply with US legislation[1]: never use deceptive headers, from names, reply-to addresses, or subject lines.

Always provide an unsubscribe link. The unsubscribe link must work for at least 30 days after sending.

To address these issues most marketeers will seek to use a third-party provider of email marketing solutions which not only avoids having to use Microsoft for the despatch of your emails, but also allows a much more professional and visual email to be provided.

As a first step you'll need to decide on a suitable email marketing package. Choosing an off the shelf email package at this stage is the recommended route to market, unless your business is already operating a customer relationship management (CRM) software system that already incorporates email marketing into the package.

Relatively simple to use cloud-based systems are easy to find online. Some of these providers offer a very basic free service up to a maximum number of recipients; others offer a free trial period but mostly with limited features.

Typical of the suppliers offering web-based email marketing solutions are Benchmark, Campaigner, Campaign Monitor, Constant Contact, Dotmailer, Force24, Freshmail, GetResponse, GraphicMail, iContact, MailChimp, VerticalResponse, Sendinblue, HubSpot and a number of other providers.

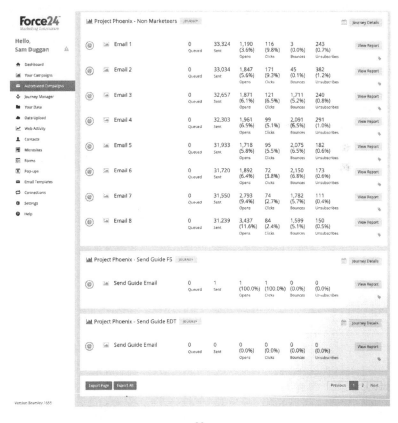

For clients based in the UK and Europe I would recommend Force24 based in the UK because of its legal compliance with all data protection legislation, and it is also ISO 27001 registered. As a first step work out the type of marketing message needed, the format you would like to send them and then decide on the email marketing platform that best fits your requirements. As you will find when you look at the different suppliers' websites some of the email marketing tools are very different. The solutions offered come with various support selections, contact management features and ultimately costs. The suppliers' pricing is normally based around the number of subscribers, and the volume of emails sent out each month.

You should check the suppliers' promotional text to ensure that the chosen package and pricing plan provides the features needed. Some of the suppliers will provide plenty of expansion opportunities within the plan agreed, but some other providers may expect you to upgrade to a pricier solution.

As your requirements are B2B, it is unlikely that you will need to communicate initially with more than a few thousand contacts until you exhaust your initial database.

Some of the service providers like Force24 can provide custom-designed templates for your business, and support training which can take away a lot of the stress of running an ongoing digital campaign. Providers offer a multitude of payment methods ranging from payment in advance to a monthly retainer offered by the likes of Force24.

As recommended in the earlier chapter on getting accurate data, target database contacts should be bought from a reputable supplier and then further researched as earlier outlined to ensure that you are talking to or emailing relevant sales prospects. However, developing that database further requires a proactive campaign to look for additional data. This could involve permission marketing, blogging or using a third-party website monitoring supplier who will gather email addresses on companies visiting your website. Getting additional sales leads will be covered in more detail in one of the subsequent chapters.

You must include your physical mailing address. However, if you are using a no frills provider like MailChimp, whilst they will try and ensure that you legally comply, this could get problematic for European based clients because they are registered in Atlanta and therefore can only comply with the GDPR by signing up to the voluntarily EU/US Privacy Shield.

It should be noted that advances in technology based around spam filters versus more sophisticated email servers can restrict the number of delivered emails giving read receipts to as few as 15% of the intended recipients.

Assuming 50% of the recipients don't give read receipts, this means that your emailer only reaches 30% of the intended targets.

If this were a consumer-based campaign it might be acceptable but for B2B marketing where there will be a finite number of relevant recipients, this means on a target list of potential customers which could be as little as 100 names, only 30 of these may receive your emailer. Supplementary routes to market should also be considered, such as posting to those targets where the target list is initially very small and who persistently just don't read any digital communications.

In a B2B marketing niche environment where there are very limited targets, for best results email marketing must always be used to support and reinforce other integrated marketing and NOT as a standalone lead generating solution without phone calls.

As outlined in the earlier chapter on 'Getting Accurate Data,' some of the database providers can only provide email addresses with a large percentage of generic addresses such as info@ or mail@ and therefore further phone research should be undertaken to identify the person responsible for your

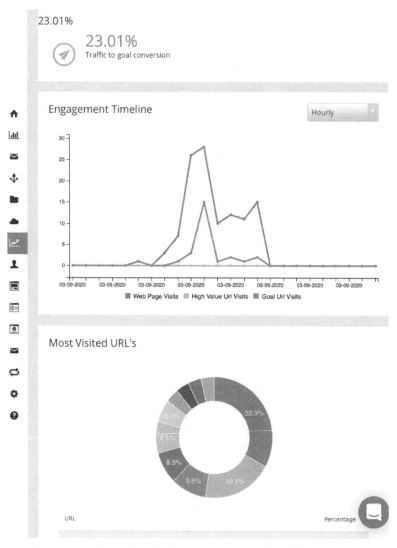

product or service. This is the person you should target, not the receptionist who opens the generic email enquiries.

Ultimately, you should end up with a database comprising your company's own prospects, some data purchased from a database provider and possibly some data from a third party such as a trade association (with permission), dealer principal or some other relevant source.

Ideally the data needs checking for duplicates and accuracy, as there is nothing worse than contacting someone who passed away two years ago!

For the purpose of this book any subsequent reference about email service providers will be based on Force24 as I have audited the company and it is based in the UK. However, all of the other suppliers already mentioned are capable of providing a suitable platform to meet the needs of most B2B campaigns.

Remember, your marketing campaign at this stage requires the ability to email a number of prospects for subsequent follow-up within 24 hours by telephone. Later in the marketing campaign we'll need to send your prospects an e-newsletter to keep them engaged but at this stage the emphasis is putting together a relatively simple typical 200-word letter.

Key points and actions you need to take from this chapter

1 - Digital is a key component of integrated marketing. Advances in email marketing allow certain platform providers like Force24 to provide automated storyboards to be set up and set out at pre-set times

2 - Understand the difference between e-marketing letters, e-blasts, e-newsletters and storyboards

3 - For the best response digital marketing needs to be used as part of integrated marketing

4 - Decide on a provider that can offer additional support such as designing templates

5 - If you are emailing letters of introduction or an offer, please try and telephone follow-up on the same day

1 Can spam Act 2003

Chapter 6

Producing digital marketing material that engages with the reader

Producing engaging digital content needs to be done as part of integrated marketing and not just as standalone material if your business is to repeat the benefits of a fully combined campaign.

The future of marketing is currently very much focused around sophisticated email campaigns but don't take my word for it, listen to the wise. Len Shneyder, VP Industry Relations, SparkPost says: "Email volume will grow. Legitimate email volume is, like our universe, always expanding for the foreseeable future." Kraig Swensrud of Campaign Monitor says: "Anyone can now create beautiful, professional email campaigns with drag-and-drop technology." Simon Cave of Stampelia says: "If you don't keep up with email marketing trends, you will find yourself overwhelmed and leave money on the table." Adam Oldfield from Force24, a UK market leader says: "We continue to invest and develop our Platform, email delivery perfection using graphics, storyboards, text and a combination of each is our sole objective no matter what the barriers, we will never become complacent."

As emphasised earlier in this book, in a perfect marketing world direct human interaction would be the best way of generating new work in the business community, but reaching large numbers of potential customers in person is virtually impossible due to time restraints, artificial barriers like efficient receptionists and the logistical costs of doing so. Therefore, to supplement other marketing activities all prospects should be receiving some kind of regular e-communication which should be part of the seven touches needed to convert a prospective customer into a customer.

These email documents need creating for integrated marketing comprise in essence a series of email storyboards, e-marketing letters with graphics, e-blast templates and e-newsletters, the latter to remind prospects and existing customers that you are a successful business.

At the start of integrated marketing an email marketing letter is needed, or if you prefer a more sophisticated approach use a series of digital storyboards. To keep things simple at this stage, let's look at the construction of the e-letter in a bit more detail.

The e-letter does not need to be complicated but should explain why you have emailed the sales prospect, what your company offers and why the product or service would be of benefit to the recipient. It should also include your contact details and you should make clear in the e-marketing letter that you will be contacting the sales prospect in a day's or couple of days' time. The e-letter should include a link to your website and any other reference sites that might be of interest to the reader such as customer testimonials. To support the e-letter you should either upload a product leaflet to your e-marketing provider, some of these suppliers like Force24 allow you to do this and then create a hyperlink to it embedded in your e-marketing document, or upload a leaflet to another site such as your website or a Force24 microsite, connected via a hyperlink.

A draft e-marketing letter (which can also be posted if you insist!) is shown on the adjoining page, note that anything that needs saying must be included on one side of A4, if your text won't fit cut it down or find someone to redraft your text to make it fit. Don't ramble in the letter, cut to the chase by telling them why you have emailed them, what your firm offers, any relevant experience in the prospective customer's target sector and why they should deal with your firm. Close the letter by advising the prospect that you'll be following up the correspondence during the next couple of days. Include within the e-marketing letter hyperlinks to your website, literature and, if you have them available, a couple of client testimonials.

If you wish to do the same through storyboards, you'll be putting across the same messages through say five emails which will use graphics and text content to present the same information in snippets of content. Normally each storyboard has a purpose, such as the basic proposition, call to arms, why the customer should engage, third party endorsements, any warranties etc. These will need to be sent out in sequence over around ten days, so your follow-up will be on day 11.

E-marketing platforms are great for monitoring the response by anyone clicking hyperlinks and if anyone clicks to your website or accesses the leaflet, you'll be able to discover this from logging into the likes of Force24 and looking at their dashboard which is part of the control panel.

The industry B2B average for potential customers clicking hyperlinks is relatively small and anything above 1% should be seen as very successful.

The small number of potential customers who have clicked the hyperlinks should be treated as a phone call priority because they clearly have an interest in your products or service. When you do make contact play it cool and don't under any circumstances tell the prospect that you have noticed that they have visited your website because this could really spook them.

We'll be revealing more detail about following up sales prospects in a later chapter, but at this point I just want to emphasise that whether you do it yourself, employ someone from a temping agency or get another colleague to do the work, it is ultra-important that everyone emailed gets a prompt phone call. If you put off the calls for any more than a few days, the target prospect won't remember even getting your e-marketing or postal letter!

To send after your e-letter and its subsequent phone follow-up, you'll also need the popular but misunderstood business communication tool, the e-marketing newsletter.

The e-marketing newsletter is a great way of staying in contact with existing and potential sales prospects and it replaces the old company newsletter that many larger firms used to regularly post.

E-newsletter styles and template formats vary hugely as does the success of these e-newsletter marketing campaigns. In the B2B sector accurate targeting remains a genuine concern because companies often don't take enough care with sourcing and then re-verifying database information.

At this stage of integrated marketing I would pick something relatively straightforward to start with, in essence nothing fancy. All of the e-marketing providers offer readymade templates that can be most easily customised to suit your newsletter requirements.

The e-newsletter can easily be populated with your business's logo, address and of course content. As the e-newsletter template will be the last thing you circulate within the quarter, as highlighted in the PR section of this book the contents can be based around any case studies, press releases and other text you have written during the earlier part of the quarter.

If you struggle with using e-templates for the e-letter, e-newsletter, storyboards or e-blast don't worry as you are not alone as most users of e-marketing websites are self-taught including the author of this book.

A nice feature of Force24 and some other providers is drag and drop and easy HTML editing which means you don't need a degree in IT to produce meaningful and attractive material. That said as with most things practice makes perfect and I would advise that you initially start with simple ready to populate designs, which are provided free by the likes of Force24.

Once you have a draft design and content please get someone to independently proof read it as there is nothing worse than having material with spelling and serious grammar mistakes.

Most e-marketing providers allow users to import their

data into an incorporated database and as a bonus only allows the same name to be imported once. This provides a level of database clean-up but of course does nothing if the initial data is hopelessly out of date.

Once everything is in place start your first campaign by sending out the e-marketing letter or a postal letter to the first fifty or 100 prospects (not existing customers).

Each sales prospect needs following up and that work should start almost immediately with the first outbound calls going out within a day of the e-letter getting circulated or if posted within 48 hours. Let's take a look at maximising your return.

Providing you have targeted the right companies and identified the correct contact at each company and have a relevant proposition that will provide some kind of demonstrable benefit to each firm, the next challenge is to reach each sales prospect with a tangible follow-up discussion. The next chapter is critical to the success of your campaign, in fact it is so important but also straightforward that I want you to read it twice.

Key points and actions you need to take from this chapter

1 - All digital content should be part your integrated marketing and the messaging should be consistent

2 - The starting point for integrated marketing is an email letter

3 - Keep your text to a maximum of a page and a bit shorter if possible

4 - Monitor the delivery figures to see which open rates and click-throughs provide the best result

5 - Use template designs provided by your provider for newsletters if possible as it avoids reinventing the wheel

Chapter 7

Websites, understanding different builders, using WordPress, communicating with your target audience and using plugins

A good website must be at the center of integrated marketing - it is one of the most critical components and the next few chapters are devoted to making it work properly for your business. You don't need to have any special technical skills and I am not expecting you to build your own website, but I am aiming to arm you with a good understanding of what kind of website you need so that you can confidently deliver integrated marketing.

The first website was built in 1991 by Tim Berners-Lee who believes that the goal of the Web is to serve humanity. He said: "We build it now so that those who come to it later will be able to create things that we cannot ourselves imagine." He went on to say: "Anyone who has lost track of time when using a computer knows the propensity to dream, the urge to make dreams come true and the tendency to miss lunch."

This chapter and the four succeeding ones are all devoted to giving you a solid grounding so that you can confidently brief your current website provider or a new website supplier to deliver exactly what your business needs rather than what the supplier wants to sell you!

This doesn't mean that website suppliers are not well intentioned, it is just that they are not experts in your business and may also have far more experience of building business to consumer sites, which are generally more brand driven, more graphical and are aimed at much bigger mass markets, so have far less experience of niche marketing.

At the time of writing there are multiple different website building solutions (sometimes called website builders). Many of these are aimed at the DIY sector and if that is what you want to do, then I can recommend Squarespace which has readymade templates and you can also import your own; HostGator which has an impressive drag and drop builder at your disposal, so that users can quickly build a website; or Wix. The latter has an ecommerce functionality, site booster and visitor analytics. If you are wanting to sell a large number of items online then you should consider Shopify which is an ecommerce website builder platform aimed at those wish to sell online. There are a large number of other website building solutions all offering a variation on a theme, and reviews can easily be found online.

All of these solutions will allow you to put together a professional looking site, with unique graphics if you have some externally designed for your new website. Alternatively, you can use one of the inbuilt templates to create a professional site, but if you do the latter you may end up with the same site graphics used by other similar companies to your own! Payment for hosting tends to be monthly, sometimes in dollars and the providers enable easy upgrades and provide a number of features as part of the package. The big downside is that you can never move your website to another hosting provider if you are unhappy with the service. Therefore, if you ever want to leave you will have to rebuild your website from scratch.

If you have outsourced your website building or plan to, then it is likely that your provider will be building the site using one of WordPress, Joomla or Drupal. These are more technically complex packages and are actually content management systems (CMS), that allow the website builder to link together the different components. CMS driven solutions are far more flexible and can be built to provide precisely what is needed, even if that means writing certain actions required using computer code like PHP.

Some over-enthusiastic marketeers and business owners do build their own CMS websites, and learn a lot from the process, however, if you have the resources outsource it to a competent website provider or unless you are technical, choose one of the easier DIY solutions. All three CMS based solutions highlighted and a number of others can provide stunning websites.

Joomla is considered an easy-to-use CMS that comes with a built-in intuitive dashboard. It also provides the option to use many third-party integration solutions. Since this is open source coding, the elements are customisable to suit your business needs. However, getting everything to function is a steep learning curve and may need some external support.

Drupal is considered to be one of the most popular open-source content management systems on the market. Its key advantages include flexibility, functionality, customisation and a wide choice of plugins. However, it requires a good in-depth knowledge of installation and modification to make it work properly.

Lastly is WordPress, which powers around 32.3%[1] of all websites on the internet. The widespread use of WordPress is due to a number of factors including the fact that it was an early adopter and is a free open source, not for profit solution provided by WordPress.org.

WordPress does not require any coding skills (but you do need to have some IT skills), has a high level of functionality and comes with a vast choice of plugins (pre-built apps) to suit a vast array of applications. Like the different packages included in the DIY listing, WordPress is available with a large number of themes which can be customised because a lot of them come with their own control panel allowing users to upload logos, change colours and add or edit wording.

For the purposes of this book WordPress is the chosen platform because of its easy to use SEO ability, flexibility, portability allowing your firm to change hosting companies and choice of plugins. In effect if you have an idea for something, you can probably find a WordPress plugin to do it. WordPress uses a large amount of HTML, CSS and a little Javascript for various aspects of its performance.

Websites need care in planning and your website needs to be in sync with integrated marketing and built around the keywords to reach your target customers; see the subsequent SEO chapter for more details.

In a nutshell, planning involves the different ways of communicating your website's content, agreeing the objectives, defining the audience and agreeing a domain name, which may be different to your company's name.

This planning part breaks into the following components:

- Who is our audience and what type of website graphics will appeal to them?

  This needs carefully thinking about, most B2B firms are slightly behind the curve, so likely in many cases to be a bit conservative. So, you might want to have more conservative colours such as blue rather than pastel or fluorescent colours. If you are not sure take a look at a few of the websites of the companies you wish to target, as you'll get a much better understanding of the culture involved.

- What is the reach of your website: national, subcontinents, worldwide, English speaking, Spanish - Latin America, Chinese or even Russian? If you are targeting different countries you will most likely need language options on the site, these can be set up to auto detect using an API (application programming interface), which reacts to the IP address location of the computer's browser.

- A rough estimate of how many products or services you will be showing (further pages can easily be added later) and do you intend to sell goods and/or services online?

- What type of navigation structure do you want for your

website - interactive, sidebar static, parallax powered, hamburger, footer, drop downs (traditional and most popular in B2B), multimedia based or centred layout?

- Website template designs
- Third party links such as LinkedIn, Facebook, Twitter and YouTube
- Any special apps that need to be added such as planning programmes like a pre-machine build or inspection
- Online commerce for selling via the website, if required
- Estimated number of pages needed to accommodate everything - you may want to delay finalising this until you have had a site map prepared.

The type of website navigation used has a big impact on conversions into enquiries and sales, and also bounce rates, the latter of which your site needs to minimise. Just remember if website visitors can't work out where to find what they require, they'll quickly depart. As a rule of thumb your website navigation should enable your potential customer to land on any page of your website and find what they require within three mouse clicks.

It would also be great if you knew that every visitor would start on your homepage and follow a predictable path but that is not how it will happen. This is because website visitors will be in many cases driven to specific content due to the other integrated marketing we'll be undertaking such as tweeting or posting on social media particular page links, pointing your company's newsletter at specific content and also adding website links to advertising content like Google Ads and LinkedIn.

It is common practice to draw a site map list of the different pages like the illustration below:

The next step is to get someone to create the website templates, this is the artwork that shows the distinct design of your site. You can at this point pick one of the website themes

A Simple Website Map

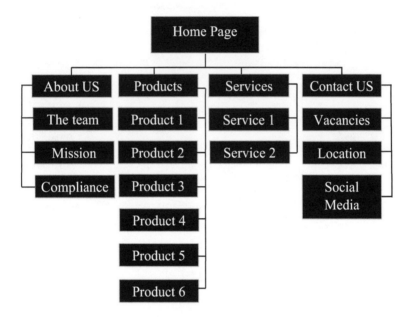

offered by either WordPress or one of the third-party vendors who specialise in selling themes. However, if you pick an off the shelf set of themes, other firms will be using them and there may be some functionalities that are not available such as linking to other levels of your website without having some special coding written.

Distinct templates will be needed for the following:
- Home page
- About Us page
- Product page
- Any third-party integration pages
- Contact page
- Any other pages that need a distinct template, such as news

Getting the right templates is very much trial and error and if you are using a web agency or design company you should get designs that are bespoke to your business with the functionality needed. However, the key is to give them a good brief based on which B2B companies you would like to target with the website, along with the earlier information you have prepared as part of this planning process.

Be prepared to modify or have your web agency modify the templates until you are satisfied. If you don't get this right at the start it will nag away at you and once the artwork has been created in HTML, it will cost more money and delay the building of your website if you subsequently want the templates changing. In my own business, despite warning clients at the outset, it is not uncommon for the templates to be approved, only to find that after converting the artwork into HTML some unseen director requests a redesign!

Once the artwork is approved, the different pages can be created based on the earlier site map you and/or the web agency have created.

All HTML templates created should be responsive templates, this makes the layout effectively fluid to provide optimal viewing on almost any device including desktop computers, Macs, tablets, laptop computers, smartphones and all other mobile devices.

It works by detecting the type of device the person is browsing with and then shrinks or expands image widths, fonts etc to provide the best possible visitor experience.

There are a number of components that need to come together to make the website work at maximum performance and I have listed each of the key ones below:

The domain name is one of the most important components because it is part of the website's optimisation. There are big advantages in having a high-quality domain name. A relevant quality domain name will not only protect your brand and make you look more professional, it also improves your website's search engine ranking, will generate new traffic and it is financially a virtual asset. This means you should be thinking about a B2B name that reflects the products or services sold. For example, a family name may have nostalgia for those working for it but does it cut the ice 200 miles or even 2,000 miles away?

So, the right B2B domain name for our fictional food machinery company might be 'The Food Machinery Company' rather than 'Jones & Co.'

Whilst most of the most successful domain names have been snapped up in the B2C sector, there are still good domain names to be obtained for the B2B sectors.

Think carefully before you purchase a domain name because apart from the actual name you might want to consider what end suffix you want. Trading internationally you should consider .com, for mainly the UK: .co.uk, just Australia: .com. au and Canada: .CA and New Zealand: .NZ should all be fine.

There are a number of domain name suppliers including GoDaddy, 123-Reg, Domain.com, Bluehost, HostGator, Namecheap, DreamHost, Shopify, Aust Domains and BuyDomains to name but a few.

My recommended UK supplier is 123-Reg because they are easy to deal with and the domain names are simple to purchase and subsequently manage through a portal which is easy to set up. For clients in the US and Canada I'd look at GoDaddy and in Australia and New Zealand Aust Domains.

Hosting a WordPress website can also be done by a number of the domain name suppliers such as 123-reg, BlueHost or GoDaddy, however it doesn't really matter so you could purchase your domain name from one supplier and host with another.

Many suppliers offer dedicated web hosting solutions which can vary from expensive dedicated servers to low cost budget shared hosting. Ideally, unless your business already has a shared or dedicated external server with a supplier such as

AWS in California, UKFast or HostPapa in Australia with spare server space and someone to set up your website, you would be better going with one of the dedicated WordPress hosting providers such as BlueHost, 123-Reg or 1&1 IONOS.

If you do decide to host on existing server space, it is important to ensure your WordPress website is placed on a high-speed server, and that it is running the latest versions of any software, so for WordPress the server needs to be running the latest version of PHP, MySQL or MariaDB and HTTPS to support (SSL).

Whichever supplier is picked, the key thing is to have one that can provide fast page loading, as otherwise it will impact on your SEO due to extra bandwidth needed for responsive templates. This normally happens when people chose low cost website hosting which can result in not achieving optimal loading speed, due to limited bandwidth.

In summary no matter how small or big your business, please don't be attracted to getting the lowest cost option, which typically might be a collective hosting plan.

Some of these suppliers offer so called value add-on SEO packages, from experience these packages do very little to generate new business as the solutions are very generic and not designed for the type of niche integrated marketing this book is advocating. Therefore, whilst you might be bamboozled by impressive graphics, these packages will have little impact and are consequently a waste of your resources.

Whether you are targeting different countries or just one country, have your website provider install W3 Total Cache as it improves the SEO and user experience of the website by increasing your website performance. This is achieved by reducing the website's load times, according to the developers, by leveraging features like content delivery network (CDN) integration and the latest best practices.

It is important that your new website is safe and secure and therefore insist on getting your website supplier to take you through what is proposed - or if you are doing it yourself you should read the next few paragraphs very carefully.

A hacked WordPress website can cause serious damage to your reputation and can even in extreme cases be used to distribute spam and send malware to your current and potential customers.

In extreme circumstances, you could even end up paying ransomware to hackers just to regain ownership of your own website. Hacking often occurs due to plugins not being regularly updated or because hackers continually target the site (almost like a game) to force entry – so do ensure your website provider has a policy for regularly updating plugins. To protect your website please ensure that the standard WordPress logon name is changed from Admin to something more complicated. A strong password should also be added that is unique for your website. Restrict those in your internal team with access and ensure that they understand the need for tight security. You should also ensure that staff remotely accessing from home have adequate security/protection on personal devices before being permitted to log on.

Insist on your website provider installing a security plugin such as Wordfence which includes an endpoint firewall and malware scanner or Sucuri™ Security. Both providers offer a free version which is adequate or a more sophisticated paid for version which allows you to block countries or even specific IP addresses from trying to logon.

In addition, using one of the managed WordPress hosting services also provides a more secure platform for your website. Managed WordPress hosting companies often offer automatic backups and WordPress updates – however be careful if you are running bespoke templates that these don't get affected by any changes. Many of these providers can also offer more advanced security configurations to help protect your website from unauthorised access.

SSL Certificates are a kind of digital certificate that authenticates websites and provides an encrypted connection. The certificate communicates to potential customers that the web hosting provider has demonstrated ownership of your website's domain. When correctly installed on a web server, an SSL certificate activates the padlock and the https protocol and allows secure connections from a web server to a browser.

Optimisation – please see the next chapter, which is devoted to this topic.

I am going to give the last words of this complicated but important chapter to Berners-Lee who said: *"We can't blame the technology when we make mistakes."*

Key points and actions you need to take from this chapter

1 - Understand the difference between DIY website building and CMS systems, then determine what system you need

2 - Work through the planning section carefully

3 - Make sure that whatever solution you go for has responsive templates

4 - Choose your domain carefully, which will be the most effective for SEO purposes

5 - Ensure that whoever hosts your website can provide adequate bandwidth and a backup facility

6 - Make sure your site has an annual SSL certificate and a security plugin

1 https://www.wpbeginner.com/why-you-should-use-wordpress/

Chapter 8

SEO: why it is better to optimise for nine keywords rather than 90

Search engine optimisation (SEO) is a much misunderstood subject. It is full of jargon ranging from terms such as black hat SEO which attempts to deceive the search engines like Google (the description originated from cowboy films where the bad guys wore black hats and the goodies white) to meta descriptions (used to list a page's content, which the search engines then show in their search results) to on-page which relates to the content and HTML source code of a webpage that can be optimised.

British musician, composer and singer Dhani Harrison described websites as kind of useless. He said: "There is so much great web content and design out there, but the ways in which they are being experienced are not being maximised." Harrison may have a valid point because if your site doesn't have a great reach how can people find it!

I will try and keep this chapter as jargon free as possible but it is still going to be a bit of a techie chapter as I need you to be able to understand how SEO works. This will then enable you, if necessary, to confidently delegate the work out to your favourite marketing agency or web development company in the knowledge that you have correctly tasked them with what you want to achieve and, just as importantly, can subsequently audit their work. Ultimately, the website is integral to integrated marketing, so the website needs to work hard to link with all the other activities.

There is a belief that websites can be optimised for hundreds of words but in fact for the average sized B2B site there is an infinite list of words that can be on-page optimised. If there were no limitations on what can be optimised there would be little opportunity for the likes of Google, LinkedIn, Facebook, Twitter and many other platforms to promote paid for backlinks, adverts and other promotional opportunities to help companies gain website traction in order to attract business - and for the likes of Google through its Ads programme to make a few dollars in the process.

As you will have seen from the earlier chapters, for the purposes of this book we have used WordPress as the standard for website building and promoting. However, it doesn't really matter for SEO purposes as most websites can be optimised although, depending on the website building platform used, there may be some limitations as to what can be done to promote the site around certain keywords.

Search engine optimising the website breaks down into a number of components including on-page content, technical optimisation and third-party links. For now, I am going to talk about on-page content and we'll talk about off-page content and backlinks later in this chapter.

Getting everything to match and work can be a real challenge, think about it like going for a formal job interview wearing pink shoes, brown trousers, a dark blue top, red eyebrows and your hair coloured green – some interviewers may be prejudiced and so it is with websites and search engines. Therefore, no matter how good your products and service, unless everything is coordinated and in sync the big search engines may give you a poor ranking.

The keywords and phrases need to be agreed at the outset to match with the words and search terms your potential customers are likely to search for, and these words also need to be in sync with the integrated marketing campaign. This is where website builders often go wrong, because if they don't know your business very well, they can set the site up for the wrong words and even the wrong geographical reach. One of my clients, based in Perth, Australia and who exports specialist industrial equipment worldwide was disappointed to discover that his website had no traction beyond the local vicinity of his business. When he raised it with the then website builder, he was told that's ok, there must be lots of people in Perth wanting your equipment!

The starting point is to ensure your website has been set up for optimisation. If you are using WordPress you will need to have installed, unless it has already been done at the time the site was built, an SEO Plugin. There are various suppliers although I would recommend Yoast as it is relatively simple to use. As a bonus the Yoast SEO plugin will automatically create for the website an XML sitemap which helps the search engines to quickly find your pages and start ranking them. Yoast also allows you to optimise each page.

The next step is to determine which keywords, descriptions, URLs, page headers and on-page content is needed to get your website in front of the right people.

There is an element of constant evaluation needed as some words will perform better than others for various reasons, the most important one being that people are using the actual search phases.

One of the cheapest ways of discovering which phases people use is to open a Google Ads account. This will not cost anything but it will allow you to check keywords to see if what you're wanting to use as a search term has internet search traction.

There are always play-offs between the words you think are needed and the terms your potential customers are searching. For example, one of my clients wants to promote feeders: the business distributed friction feeders but the client thought it would be better just to promote feeders. A Google Ads search for friction feeders found that it generates around 200 per month, but a search for just the word feeders found that around 2,000 people a month search for this word. In effect for every valid search the client generated 10 were invalid, which resulted in a high level of page bounce.

Google does not like to see high levels of page bounce rates and wrongly assumed that people were disenchanted with the on-page content and lowered the client's overall page ranking. This presented the client with the double problem of poorly thought out content as far as Google was concerned and, secondly, the attraction of the wrong type of people, some of whom were looking to purchase bird feeders.

Using Google Ads or another key search tool like SEMrush, will help to determine the best words and phrases which should be the starting point to deciding which of your words and phrases will deliver the best results. These keywords need to match up with the overall theme of your integrated marketing campaign agreed earlier within this book.

Armed with some of your keywords and phrases, work should now start on the optimisation. The key thing is to start with say five per page and build from there, further variants can be added later.

At this point I should stress that this book is very much about arming you with a strong overview as I am not anticipating that many readers will have the patience and skillsets to want to do all the work themselves, but marketers must have a decent overview, so some of the key actions have been abbreviated.

In Yoast and on many other website SEO packages there is an opportunity to provide a brief site description. As a starting point you will need to create this description about the site, this needs to say something very relevant so for our fictional food machinery company it might be food machinery or, if insurance, insurance for the food industry.

The key thing is to focus on what matters. There is no point in attracting thousands of people to the site all wanting car insurance if you sell trade food insurance, as this will create a high site bounce rate and will downgrade the website's ranking!

The SEO process normally starts with the creation of friendly URLs which are like a page anchor within your overall website which enable the search engines to find your page. SEO friendly URLs contain words that clearly explain the content of the page, and they're easy to read by both humans and search engines.

An SEO friendly URL for our food insurance company should be like this: https://www.smeinsurance.com/food-and-drink-insurance/

Note that the URL includes food and drink insurance. It doesn't matter what your industry is about but do use the keywords for the specific page within the url if you can.

Secondly you need to look at the header tags, these are important because they tell the search engines what your website page is about. Header tags are simply the page header (H1), then the H2 tag is a subheading and should contain similar keywords to your H1 tag. The H3 is then a subheading for H2 and so on.

Search engines will recognise the copy in your header tags as more important than the rest. This always starts with your H1 and works its way down in importance to the H2, H3 and so on. These tags will help support the overall theme or purpose of the website page.

It is important that these headers contain the keywords for that particular page because the search engines will crawl the site and will pick up on the headers and should recognise these keywords as important.

The on-page content should also have your key phrases interwoven but not too repetitively as there is a fine balance between getting the right level of repetition and swamping the page. Fortunately, Yoast also allows you to add a keyword or phrase for each page and provides a level of analysis in terms of five words or phrases you have used within the body of the copy. The number of words used on each page is also important and around 600 words per page is currently considered optimal for

SEO. Websites with less than 300 words per page are considered "thin" by Google and this may affect the page ranking.

Ensure that every website page provides unique content, don't copy and paste any of the content from other pages. Each page will also need a meta description, this is a snippet of up to about 155 characters which summarises a page's content and is used by the search engines like Google to show the content when someone searches for a specific phrase.

Pictures on the website should be individually named and also given alternative descriptions. Picture 1 and picture 2 are not acceptable and should be give the correct product or service name. All images should also be optimised for Google (compressed) as large images cause a drag on the Google servers and may as a consequence downgrade your site's ranking.

If you are still with me thank you, and once again apologies about the level of technical content.

This moves us on to the final topic: backlinks. Backlinks are hyperlinks from other websites and domains that point to some content on your own website.

Backlinks are a vote of confidence in your website and help to strengthen the overall relevance and content of a website. The more relevant website backlinks a site can achieve, generally the better the ranking. Therefore, the more applicable and unique content your website has, the greater the number of backlinks it is likely to attract.

Search engines use backlinks to help determine the importance of a page and website. Traditionally, the likes of Google used the number of backlinks to determine the popularity of certain pages. This has changed and backlinks are now evaluated using a number of industry related ranking factors; this has created a move away from volume to the quality of the sites from which the links are originating.

One of the factors used in this equation to determine the popularity of a site is an algorithm - or as the search engines call it, PageRank (PR), named after a Google founder Larry Page. This is utilised by Google Search to rank web pages in their search engine results. One of these results is dwell time, the actual time a visitor spends on your website.

This is where integrated marketing comes into its own if you know how to do it, because items like newsletter content can be linked to your website so that when someone reads your published newsletter via Force24 or one of the other automated marketing platforms, it hyperlinks back to your website where the core content should be posted. Consequently, people reading your newsletter via your website will have an increased dwell time, this will impress Google and should help to improve the site's ranking.

Other options to create easy backlinks originate from media like Twitter where story links can be tweeted out, plus Facebook hyperlinks, LinkedIn and other social media platforms that are relevant to your business (see chapter 17 for more details). Don't forget to include hyperlinks into any PR material you circulate as some publishers will leave these in, instantly boosting the impact of your PR story through funnelling visitors back to your website.

There are lots of other opportunities to create backlinks but before you get too carried away you should only encourage links on sites relevant to your business, as obscure sites can create bad links which can actually downrank your website - sorry to spoil the party. Relevant links would be incoming links to your website from trade associations, website forums to do with your industry, relevant online directories, satisfied clients, digital publications, third party trade blogs and external blogs that you have created and then linked, plus the inclusion of material posted on social media.

As part of this process your business needs to monitor the backlinks your website is generating. This allows you to verify that the outreach is working. Secondly, you can then monitor if you pick up any risky backlinks. As an example, links from domains originating from Brazil and Russia can be notorious creators of spam. It is possible to reject links from sites coming from certain parts of the world through Google Search Console (see the next chapter), preferably as soon as you find them to prevent them having any impact on your website.

You should also consider having some outbound links but preferably not to the same connections providing your website with inbound links.

Companies like Yoast feel very strongly about this because they see their mission as SEO for everyone. Yoast says: "We strongly believe in equal chances for everyone on a connected web. By asking you to add that outbound link, we ask you to connect your website to the next website. And that website to the next website.

"By doing so, we create a web that expands and expands, from one related website to another. We help Google to connect the dots. We help Bing to get insights on what sites or better what pages relate to each other."

Once complete the website should be submitted (or resubmitted) to the top three search engines Google, Bing and Yahoo for crawling. Whilst Google and some of the others will probably find your site, this could take a while so it is better to be certain.

Lastly, do please install Google Analytics so that you can get a regular report on the number of visitors to your website, where they originate from and which pages they visited, and for how long. Installing Google Analytics, which is free, is relatively simple: it just needs some code inserting near the top of each page before any other script or CSS tags on your website. However, I would recommend using Google Analytics in conjunction with some of the other providers like SEMrush which is an optimisation tool.

Key points and actions you need to take from this chapter

1 - Don't randomly pick your keywords, start with a shortlist and research them through something like Google Ads, these words also need to be consistent with your integrated marketing campaign

2 - Install an optimisation plugin like Yoast

3 - Ensure everything on your website gets optimised including images, urls, headers and meta descriptions

4 - Avoid mixed messages by ensuring all the onsite optimisation matches the keywords

5 - Integrated marketing – make sure PR stories have hyperlinks back to your website, use social media such as Twitter, Facebook and LinkedIn to post relevant links back to your website. The core content for newsletters should be posted on your website and hyperlinked to the newsletter, allowing visitors to read the stories on your website to increase dwell time

6 - Make sure you submit the site to Google, Yahoo and Bing

7 - Continue to evaluate the performance of your website using Google Analytics and other optimisation tools like SEMrush. Make adjustments where necessary to fine tune the SEO, which should be an ongoing process

Chapter 9

Measuring and re-evaluating the performance of your website

Measuring the performance of the website is an important part of integrated marketing because a successful campaign is likely to increase traffic to the website. Therefore, checking the success of the site should give a good indication of how your campaign is working.

Winston Churchill is credited with saying: "Success is not final, failure is not fatal, it is the courage to continue that counts." Nothing could be more so with B2B company websites and if I could only influence you to do just one thing, it would be to innovate and keep innovating your website, week in week out.

This doesn't mean recommissioning regular website rebuilds and/or rebranding work, it means putting in place some independent method of checking your website's performance and then making incremental changes to improve its performance.

Whilst regularly generating regular sales leads is a great way to monitor the performance of your firm's website, for most B2B companies we are talking niche markets and as a consequence the number of sales enquiries generated will not be massive.

Therefore, the most effective way of determining whether your website is really converting visitors into potential customers is through scrutinising website analytics or, more accurately, website metrics.

In an increasingly competitive marketplace, the use of website tools is on the rise with the use of Google Analytics because it is free, topping the list for popularity. Google Analytics is relatively easy to use and provides data on those who visit and interacted with your website. It complements Google Search Console, which is also free. Google Search Console is very much search engine driven and offers tools and insights that can assist your website's visibility and presence in the Search Engine Results Pages (SERPs).

For basic reporting I would recommend installing Google Analytics if you haven't done so already as a result of the last chapter, however I would use this in conjunction with one of the packages that works with the search engines.

In addition to Google Search Console there are a number of competing suppliers including SEMrush which I highlighted in the previous chapter and is my preferred partner. Other suppliers include Spring Metrics, Woopra, Mint and Chartbeat. All of these suppliers provide information at different levels so that you can make the adjustments necessary to your design and content.

The first action should be to decide on a partner: companies like SEMrush which can also report on the performance of your social media and are offered on a free trial.

Your next step should be to set some goals and keep a historical record of performance, otherwise any website analytics will be meaningless. It is also useful to build up a picture of the competition and how they are performing in the battle for keywords, which is where SEMrush can help because it can compare your site's performance against the competition. This is very useful although sometimes the results can come as a shock.

Website traffic and the number of visits is the normal starting point for any analysis. Whilst this type of analysis can be useful in providing an overview as to how the site is performing compared to an earlier time period, it can be difficult to establish any hard facts other than a feelgood experience or disappointment if the site is going backwards.

The key thing is to use the data to establish which pages

are attracting the most visitors and which pages need to be improved.

Using any of the packages outlined should provide useful website metrics for you to evaluate your firm's website's performance and can be breath-taking. Ultimately, you'll also need to set some initial goals after determining the current performance of the website, the point to consider is what should you be looking for beyond visitor numbers and the pages visited?

There are seven key elements (or eight if you have SEMrush) to monitor, and visitor numbers is just one of them:

1 The amount of time people spent on your website (the higher the better) and the number of times they revisited.

2 What the bounce rate is, the number of visitors who left the site after viewing just one page.

3 The number of visitors v the number of enquiries, if the first is high and the second low there could be issues with the website's content.

4 Poor visitor numbers, which could be caused by the wrong keywords, slow load time or it could be blocked because it has been left in 'do not crawl' mode setting on the WordPress Admin panel.

5 Which of your integrated marketing activities delivered the most visitor numbers and what impact did this have on overall visitor numbers?

6 Checking that the analytic metrics are working properly because if they are not set up properly the results will be slanted.

7 The level of visitor engagement: even if your visitor number are low, if there is a high level of visitor engagement this is a very good sign.

8 (optional if you have SEMrush) The performance of your website against that of your main competitors.

Results from making website changes and measuring the performance can be slow so please don't be impatient for results. Aim for incremental improvements, this means making controlled website changes rather than major changes.

Key points and actions you need to take from this chapter

1 '- Continue to innovate your website and add new content
2 - Chose a package like SEMrush to measure the performance of your website and to compare it against those of your competitors
3 - Agree some website metrics and performance benchmarks and stick with them
4 - Aim for incremental improvements, work first on the pages that are performing the worst

Chapter 10

Understanding Google and how to keep on message with this dominant search engine

It would be impossible to write a book about integrated marketing without including some detailed information about Google and how it works.

At the top of five most popular search engines is Google with a dominant worldwide market share[1] between 70.83% and 91.98%. This is followed by Bing which has a market share between 2.55% and 12.61% and, in a poor third place Yahoo with a market share between 1.66% and 2.83%. In China the most popular is Baidu with a global market share between 0.7% and 11.83% and in Russia Yandex, with a global market share between 0.45% and 1.41%.

Google's hold is all commanding whatever the device, whether tablet, desktop or mobile to access internet services. As Ehsan Sehgal, a journalist, poet and author is credited with saying: "Google, the internet world, the internet power, and the internet advantages, where, there, all the monopolies die and disappear, and the talent is visible to the globe."

Understanding a little about how Google operates is key to getting good integrated marketing results.

What made Google the most popular and trusted search engine is speed combined with quality search results. As highlighted in the preceding chapter Google uses complex algorithms to provide users with the most accurate results. At the heart of the algorithms is a simple principle that websites referenced by other websites are more important than others and therefore should be given a higher search ranking.

Google continues to develop its algorithms with the latest update taking place in 2020. These are combined with hundreds of other elements such as machine learning to provide a reliable way to discover exactly what you need on the Internet.

The importance of Google is without question, but its storage and management of data and especially personal data has on a number of occasions landed it in hot water with the European Union and some national governments.

What you need to understand is that Google operates not one or two big computer servers to provide its services, but around a million servers! This is combined with twelve big data centers. There are sometimes different servers providing the same information in different formats which can result in mismatched search results resulting in a company's website getting a high ranking on a desktop and lower on a mobile device and sometimes the reverse.

There are a number of things you can do to keep Google onside. The first is to follow Google's best practice by reading up on specific subjects via https://support.google.com.

Of particular importance is the fact that Google caches website pages and then stores a copy on its servers. This happens when its engine visits a site for indexing. According to Google there are two main versions of caches: web browser caches and proxy caches.

The first one works on the user's computer and the other one on the network and can serve one or many users. Storing this level of data requires vast storage and server processing power to quickly recall the information.

To keep Google onside you need to ensure that all images used on websites are optimized through compression to ensure the size is minimal otherwise the site will take longer to load, but of the most importance is that Google will generally reward sites that have compressed images by improving the ranking, providing you also adhere to the SEO points in the earlier chapter.

However, just remember that finding the optimal settings for your website images needs to take into account a number of factors including format capabilities, content of encoded data, quality, pixel dimensions, and a few others.

When building new websites or updating an existing site please make sure you have responsive templates and a mobile version of the website.

The search engines use bots to crawl the web to log what is on different pages. The Google web crawler is known as the Googlebot. Part of this process is to find new content and updates. So, although it might sound like common sense, if you neglect to keep your website updated with new content, it will quickly become a time capsule and Google will down-mark the site. In a competitive marketplace anything that lowers your website's ranking is not good, so keep Google happy by regularly adding more relevant content.

When websites are built there is a tick box to stop the search engines crawling the site, it is normal practice to untick this when the site goes live, the text will say something like don't let search engines crawl. Whilst this might sound obvious, I have come across a number of sites when troubleshooting for clients where the box has remained ticked and the internet has been deprived of a good website, and the client lots of new sales.

There are a number of tools to help you achieve good optimization like SEMrush and Google Search Console, previously known as Webmaster Tools. Both suppliers offer a set of tools to give website owners an opportunity to see how their content is seen by the search engines. They also provide reports and data, to better understand how your pages appear in search results. Users also get to see the actual search terms individuals are using to find your firm's website, how each page appears in the search results, and how often the pages are clicked.

Key points and actions you need to take from this chapter

1 - Try and understand how Google works and then ensure that everything you do is Google friendly

2 - Read up on specific Google topics by visiting: https://support.google.com

3 - Learn about Google Search Console and set up an account, it is free to use and should help improve the ranking of your website, consider signing up to SEMrush

1 source https://www.reliablesoft.net/top-10-search-engines-in-the-world/

Chapter 11

Taking the biscuit: the use of cookies and how to turn website visitors and those who engage on other platforms into sales leads.

Cookies help link together different digital marketing activities and rather like a bee they cross- pollinate information between diverse marketing platforms, making them an invaluable friend of integrated marketing.

The ability to track website visitors and other platforms using cookies makes them one of the most controversial marketing topics. To marketeers cookies are extremely exciting because of their ability to allow companies to track and sometimes target or retarget potential customers with specific offers. Conversely, civil liberties campaigners are very concerned, and in Europe civil liberties are winning the battle to have cookies more tightly controlled or even abolished.

Cookies were developed in the mid-1990s to assist with page loading and remembering browser sessions, enabling individuals to access the same material again when they logged onto the same website. For the record cookies are small text files that are placed on your computer by the websites, social media platforms and other links you visit or click. They are widely used in order to make websites work, or perform more efficiently, as well as to provide information to a website owner.

As a result of the ongoing development of European human rights laws, legislation has been put in place within the EU to regulate cookies. This has resulted in strict controls to regulate them within the EU, UK and also coincidentally in some parts of North America like California. At the time of writing only Australia does not yet have laws that require explicit consent before you deploy or "drop" a cookie in your website visitor's browser.

Due to the finite number of potential customers in the B2B sector, cookies play an important role in tracking prospective customers through a variety of marketing components such as newsletters and e-marketing material to determine the content read and external links clicked, to build up a report concerning the items of interest. The automated marketing platform provided by Force24 can even rank the amount of interest expressed by users into a report, that can be used to cherry pick the top-ranking sales leads.

The advertising industry has also been redefined by cookies and campaign strategies can now be created to monitor online products of interest and retarget these individuals through other platforms like LinkedIn and Facebook.

At the other extreme companies like LinkedIn, Amazon, eBay and many other big names will pay a website owner a commission in return for using the website to target people who have previously visited one of their websites. This is known as an affiliated marketing program and commission is paid for any sales subsequently generated.

In basic terms, an affiliate tracking cookie is a file that is created and stored on your visitor's web browser when they click on one of your affiliate links. This enables affiliate networks to have the ability to determine where any sales have been generated from.

Of particular significance to integrated marketing are the following:

- Identifying website visitors
- Retargeting website visitors
- The generation of sales leads from tracking the activities of newsletter recipients

The process of identifying website visitors is not perfect and whilst Google Analytics will advise on the number of visitors to a website it does not divulge the identity of the individuals. However, there are a number of companies that provide this type of service, using a system called reverse IP address lookup. Once they have identified the IP address the providers then use Facebook, LinkedIn or some other public platform to identify the individuals, whilst avoiding breaching strict EU data protection legislation, the GDPR.

There are a number of providers and these include:

- Lead Forensics – UK and USA – https://leadforensics.com
- Spotler – UK – https://spotler.co.uk
- Force24 – UK and Europe https://force24.co.uk – looks up the company but not the individual

Each provider works slightly differently: Force24 provides the service as part of its integrated automated marketing platform, whilst Lead Forensics concentrates on providing a specialist service built around just website tracking.

It is possible to retarget website visitors by putting cookie tracking on a website that communicates with a third party website or platform based on a data match. This allows through tracking cookies the ability to re-advertise a product such as a holiday, clothing or B2B service when the individual subsequently visits another website or platform like LinkedIn. This kind of LinkedIn advertising is known as website retargeting and, as the name suggests, it allows companies to target individuals who have recently visited their website. Remarketing ads developed by Facebook work to a similar format.

The generation of sales leads from tracking the activities of newsletter recipients is provided by the leading automated platform marketing providers. Most digital marketing platforms designed for circulating digital material such as newsletters, offers and other communications are designed to track visitors and monitor their activities such as areas of interest, location and type of browser. Some of these systems like the Force24 platform can rank the level of interest so marketeers can just contact the users demonstrating the greatest interest.

The legal position regarding cookies is still slightly fluid. However, in the EU and UK cookies are now regulated as part of the GDPR which requires transparency and consent if any tracking is involved. There is a duty to inform visitors if you set cookies, and also in clear language what the cookies do and why, this is known as the cookie policy. More challenging, you must also get the user's consent. Consent must be actively and clearly given. The exception to this rule applies to essential cookies used to provide online services at someone's request. For example, to remember what's in their online shopping basket, or to provide online banking security. Similar rules apply in California.

As a starting point companies will need to determine what cookies are on their website. There are a number of providers who will do this for free such as Cookiebot which will complete an audit. This provider analyses your website and emails a report to you with a complete list of all cookies used, including their purpose and type.

There are other suppliers like Cookie Policy Generator, which will even write the cookie policy for you and provide you with a pop-up banner, for a fee.

Interestingly, some of the different search engines have taken opposing stances to cookies and similar technologies; for example, Google is happy to track individuals for a variety of reasons such as accessing specific content, its own advertising and their location. Other search engines like DuckDuckGo refuse to do any tracking and the provider has built a search engine around protecting the individual's privacy, for example it does not save your search histories.

This is further complicated by some of the browser providers including Google Chrome. Many of the web browsers include some form of privacy setting, which allows the user to surf without saving cookies, temporary files or the browsing history to the computer. These settings block targeted digital advertising which can result in inconsistent campaign reports.

Before getting too carried away, I would strongly recommend that if you are in the UK you visit the Information Commissioner's Office (https://ico.org.uk) to read up on the lawful use of cookies or in the State of California the CCPA (https://oag.ca.gov/privacy/ccpa)

Key points and actions you need to take from this chapter

1 - Try and understand what cookies do and why they are controversial

2 - Appreciate their importance to integrated marketing

3 - Learn about compliance

4 - Consider how you can best deploy platforms that use cookies to track people interested in your products

5 - Understand how to use cookies to identify website visitors, retarget website visitors and get tracked leads from newsletter recipients

6 - Visit one of the regulatory authorities' websites to learn about cookies relevant to your county like the ICO or CCPA

Chapter 12

Mastering PR can generate rich dividends

Whether it is in the battlefield, factory or Westminster, battles, perceptions and reputations are made or broken through PR (public relations). PR provides the life blood and vitality to integrated marketing. It tells your story and can be colored to promote the story you want, which normally happens at the start of your integrated marketing journey.

Bill Gates once said that if he were down to his last dollar he would spend it on PR. Whilst even I wouldn't go that far it is true that PR can subtly communicate with a target audience that traditional advertising could never reach. Sustained PR can also build up a perception which is subsequently very difficult to contradict.

To win the Battle of El Alamein, General Montgomery used PR techniques to fool his German rival Field Marshall Rommel into thinking that the main attack would come from a different location. Until the British had mastered PR they never had a victory but, as Churchill subsequently remarked, after El Alamein they never had a defeat. Once allied forces had mastered PR they went on to fool the Germans again and again. In 1944 PR was used to convince Hitler that the main allied invasion force would attack Calais. So convinced was Hitler that this would be the main invasion route, he held back his top Panther tank divisions to defend Calais when they could have been used to defeat the allies in Normandy.

At boardroom level PR can make and break individuals. Gerald Ratner - then chairman, after-dinner speaker and chief executive of the Ratner Group - told the Institute of Directors in 1991 that his firm did a cut-glass sherry decanter complete with six glasses on a silver-plated tray that your butler can serve you drinks on, all for $4.95 that is total crap. His remarks were printed and broadcast to the UK nation. Some of Ratner's stock market investors panicked and sold their shares, wiping $500 million from the value of Ratner's jewelers - and soon afterwards he became the former chairman.

In the UK who can forget the duffle-coated Michael Foot on Remembrance Day, the baseball cap wearing William Hague or the bacon butty eating Ed Miliband - or the spend, spend Jeremy Corbyn in the 2019 election. Opponents used PR to portray Foot as Worzel Gummidge. Hague suffered a PR sartorial trial, Miliband was painted as out of touch and Corbyn as a useful idiot for the Kremlin. In reality Foot, Hague and Miliband all attended Oxford University and distinguished themselves before even entering politics. All four had done insufficient to protect their reputations and in each case the Government of the day set the PR agenda and used four years to hammer home their projected shortcomings.

Politics in the US is no different to the UK in how politicians are treated by the media. Take former governor of Alaska Sarah Palin as an example. To quote directly from the Guardian "Has the world known a greater horror than what it witnessed on Tuesday when Sarah Palin endorsed Donald Trump for president of the United States? I don't mean physical horror, like murders, genocide or sexual violence.

"I mean lingering existential dread, the kind of sick feeling that burns the inside of your stomach like you just drank a pint glass full of battery acid."[1]

One can only speculate how damaging the 2011 allegations that Sarah Palin snorted cocaine off a 55 gallon oil drum and allegedly had affairs with NBA star and her husband's business partner have been on her subsequent political career, and how the media has subsequently treated her. Sarah Palin had been a successful politician and business woman but that is of no consequence because the media has now developed its own narrative and it is not flattering.

However, clever politicians have been able to use PR to drown out their critics. In the US Donald Trump developed the phrase fake news to challenge the likes of the distinguished New York Times and, in Australia during the 2019 election, a news story about the Labor Party supporting a "death tax" – which turned out to be fake – gained significant traction on social media.

The phase 'public relations' has become a generic term used to define promotional activities and actions. Public relations is interpreted very differently by the diverse sectors making up the business sector and the community in general. The PR skills needed to win a war or election are very different to promoting a B2B product or service. That said, they all have one thing in common - the use of the media to build a reputation.

In a perfect marketing world, the best way of selling is to speak to customers interested in buying your product or service direct. Sadly, we don't live in marketing utopia and potential customers often have to make the first move. Just supposing that customer does make the first move and finds three websites offering the same product or service at almost the same price and delivery. Why would the customer pick your offering over those of your competitors? If your product or service is subsequently ordered, it will most likely be down to reputation.

Building a reputable reputation is down to hard work but PR can also play a decisive hand.

Just supposing your last customer, the one at the food factory who bought your product or service, can be convinced to say nice things about your business in a case study; then just supposing after he or she has approved it you can get publicity in some of the trade publications covering your target market; just supposing three other companies (possibly competitors of your customer) read the media article and find your website and place an enquiry? That is the prize from a well-executed PR campaign which is part of integrated marketing. Like it or loathe it, public relations is a key pillar of the B2B marketing community.

Good PR involves getting existing customers or clients to say nice things about your products or services. In a complex world where the internet is always a click away, people mostly still buy from people not machines. How many times have you found that dream holiday only to find your aspirations dashed by a few unhelpful comments from past holiday guests on TripAdvisor. However, please don't be fooled by the success or failure of very public consumer campaigns: carefully targeted B2B PR can really make a difference to your reputation and improve your bottom line.

Key points and actions you need to take from this chapter

1 - Battlefield, boardroom or Westminster: battles, perceptions and reputations are made or broken through PR
2 - Manage your company's reputation otherwise your competitors might do it for you
3 - Understand the concept of PR and learn to manage it
4 - You must harness PR as part of integrated marketing

1 Sarah Palin's weird and wonderful endorsement of Donald Trump, The Guardian 20/01/2016
2 Mail Online 30 November 2019

Chapter 13

Writing for the media, how to make a great PR story

B2B media related PR plays an important role in integrated marketing. This chapter is all about writing PR material which some consider is a little bit of a craft. However, whether you are reading this chapter to learn about writing or just want an overview of where it fits into integrated marketing so that you can understand what's needed, I'd urge you despite the technical nature of this chapter to read on!

B2B PR can be split into a number of categories:

Written - press releases, features, case studies, opinion pieces, white papers, blogs and social media hyperlinks to the article.

Verbal - editorial visits, editorial briefings, new facility openings and an editorial interview with your customer.

The target audience for everything listed above is the trade media read by target customers.

One of the most prized PR pieces and one of the more difficult to achieve is a case study based around your latest contract. The aim of the case study is to get your customer to describe in their own words the process they went through to select your firm as the supplier.

Your overall objective is to get your latest customer to tell all their competitors about why your company is so good, why they picked your firm as a supplier and the benefits your piece of equipment or service is bringing to their business. However, never say this to your latest customer as given what I have just said they may well be reluctant to participate. However, do tell your customer if they are supportive that you would like to arrange for them to get some free publicity which will help project them to the forefront of the industrial sector they are involved in supplying, which should help their business. Remember all of the statements in this paragraph are true but it is down to you which you emphasize.

A word of caution, many would-be case studies get mucked up and therefore not published because the customer subsequently interferes too much with the draft editorial copy and the legal department refuse to approve it.

Getting a great case study is all about getting your customer to outline a plausible process about how they went about procuring the supplier. Trying to pack the editorial with a lot of promotional advertising words will not work and is therefore best avoided. Conversely demonstrating in a case study how the supplier solved a specific production or business problem will be really valuable and should subsequently generate your business some great publicity.

For the purposes of integrated marketing, a case study is preferable but if this isn't possible a press release will suffice.

It is not the purpose of this book to teach you how to write and if English is not really your thing it might be best to secure the services of a freelance journalist, PR consultant or if your budget will stretch a PR agency. That all said, let's talk about what a case study should look like and if you are writing it or engaging someone to do it, how it can be done.

The first thing to do is to plan your content and put together some questions. One of the lead questions is obviously why did the customer choose the seller's firm?

This needs carefully explaining by the customer in his or her words and you may need to be patient and have to prompt them.

After they have been answered by your customer, the questions will need stringing together into a seamless piece of editorial comprising typically between 300 and 550 words. The writing style needs to be akin to a business page in a national newspaper and should be 1½ or double line spaced. Please avoid platitudes when describing your own business because it won't be published by most trade journals and will undermine the strength of the case study.

These are the main questions although you will need to customize them and may want to add some additional questions:

- Can you briefly describe what your company does? (Main products, how long established, how many people employed, if more than one site, please advise what site the product or service is being used at?
- What are the main benefits of the product (or service – customize as appropriate) that you have recently purchased from my business?
- What prompted the need for the investment or purchase?
- Increased sales?
- New markets so a need for different solution?
- Compliance or security issues?
- Why did you choose my company as your supplier?
- Did you consider other suppliers?
- What advantages does the product or service have over others?
- What is your opinion of both my company and the product or service that we have supplied? (Responsiveness, level of service, ease of use or access, experience)
- Did the product or service need any special changes to meet your requirements?
- Is the product or service supplied operating as a "stand alone" or as part of a collaborative or networked solution?
- What benefits has the product or service brought to your company?
- Who does your company supply - i.e., well-known brands? (are we allowed to mention customers by name or should we refer to them without using specific name?)

- Would you recommend my firm (the supplier) to another company?

Double check the name and job title of the person interviewed.

The key thing during the interview process is to encourage the customer to open up. Once recorded the next challenge is to try and pull it all together. As you will see each of the interview questions flows into the next to generate a continuous piece which, with good punctuation, can make very readable editorial.

Once drafted the case study should be checked for order of relevance and also to ensure that the first paragraph tells the story in miniature if the subsequent publishing editor only needs a very short article to fill a space.

Keep the sentences reasonably snappy and don't use three words where one will suffice. Do remember the main point of the exercise which is to showcase your business as a great supplier, described using your customer's own words.

After carefully tweaking and proof reading send the draft case study to your customer and get them to approve it. Obviously, this is their story about you so the customer must feel comfortable, so let them make changes providing it doesn't ruin the overall case study. Once approved the case study is ready for circulation, however, we'll come back to the distribution process in a short while.

If you are unable to get a case study because you haven't made a sale or are a start-up business, a press release will need to suffice. Press releases are normally a bit shorter than a case study due to the reduced content available that can be included. The press release will need to talk about why you are targeting a particular sector. In the case of our mythical editorial it will need to talk about your product or service and about your experience in supplying the target sector and/or about the benefits the equipment or service you are providing will bring to those in the sector.

As a general rule, once the PR story is told stop writing. Press releases are written and circulated to the relevant trade media to highlight a client's news/developments. The purpose of the release is to communicate with a target audience in order to build your reputation in their markets, announce news, inform customers/potential customers and generally help build their profile – well at least that's what my PR handbook says. However, case studies are more about what your customer will and won't say. Sadly, each year thousands of case studies never move beyond the initial drafting stage because the customer has subsequently got cold feet.

It should be remembered that press releases are standalone pieces of editorial and are therefore not an advert. In addition, all press releases and case studies need to have a story to tell even if the overall theme is a bit flimsy otherwise no independently minded editor will ultimately print them.

If you are drafting the story start with the fact you are targeting a particular sector such as the food sector. Your second paragraph needs to talk about the product or service and the benefits it brings. If the product or service is new to the sector, please tell the reader and whilst I would counsel against mentioning the actual cost of any product or service, I would urge you to highlight the cost savings in time or money that it will provide.

Some other companies may already be using the product or service, which they have obtained from another supplier. Whilst you can't claim credit for getting the order you can mention that the product or service is already being used by Joe Bloggs & Co.

The same rules concerning pagination apply as per the case studies. Also remember when writing any editorial to never use a mixture of British, American, Australian or Canadian words. If you are an American use Americanisms and if you are Brit, go for your best grammar. However (multi-nationals take note) mixing up the languages will be a big turnoff for editors and will result in the piece getting permanently filed in the trash bin.

As already mentioned, it is not my job to teach you to write but here are a few case study and press release editorial pointers.

Numbers should be 1 – 9 type in full i.e., nine, thereafter always numerical i.e., 10, 11, 12

Job titles should not be in capitals as they are not proper nouns, however on the basis that your customer is always right, change to suit their own style if pressed to do so.

Always singular not plural, the company, it and they are sometimes confused. A company is always it, therefore they, we and are should not be used in editorial copy. The only exception to this rule is your own quote which can be expressed in a plural format, or alternatively you are talking about a group of companies, i.e., the Rapid Group of Companies moving to London.

Sentences, ideally, they should not contain more than 30 words.

Repetition, please check that the same words are not used over and over, if necessary, look in a Thesaurus, either book or on the computer (lives in Word under tools, language) for alternatives.

Once your case study or press release (hereafter called editorial) has been drafted and if applicable approved, the next challenge is to start generating some publicity. Using integrated marketing as already highlighted, the editorial can be used to generate publicity in trade journals both print and online, Twitter, Facebook, as content for an e-newsletter and as an attachment for the direct marketing campaign. In effect that piece of editorial has a number of diverse outlets.

The starting point to getting some publicity in the trade media requires some type of media database. Most professional PR agencies and larger in-house PR departments have access to online media databases, which can be searched to identify suitable publications. However, a licensing agreement to access the databases is not cheap and most small marketing budgets can't justify spending a few thousand pounds or dollars on an annual license.

If you can afford to use a media database provider look to the likes of PRmax, CisionPoint, FeaturesExec, Gorkana or MEDIAtlas. These providers all cover the UK, US, Canada, Australia and most of the world. My own preferred partner is PRmax, which is a friendly and flexible supplier. Some of these providers will also (for an additional fee) circulate your PR material, however in the case of PRmax it is included within the subscription.

Alternatively, talk to a relevant local PR agency who might sell you a bespoke list and even do a deal on circulating your material.

Many smaller B2B firms may need to put together their own database without the help of a media list provider, due to the hefty costs involved. A good starting point is to look at the publications that your target customers are reading. Check the magazines left by potential and existing customers in their receptions. Most print magazines have an editorial contacts page, photograph the page with your smartphone for extracting into a spreadsheet later.

For illustration purposes it has been agreed that your firm is targeting the food sector, although I appreciate you could be providing raw materials to plastics manufacturers, recruitment services to the fashion industry, custodial locks to the prison service or print machines to the corrugated industry.

Frankly it doesn't really matter because a B2B media campaign will follow a very similar campaign path.

Using an outline search profile, Google the internet for additional trade magazine names and don't ignore any digital publications because they are even more important than the

more impressive print versions, due to the additional website SEO support they provide.

Using the search terms "food trade magazines UK" or "food trade magazines USA," you should start to identify relevant publications. This is a mind dulling experience because you will need to work through about ten pages on Google and record each publication's name for checking later. After exhausting this search term try and be creative with the next, try food and drink, food production, food manufacture, food trade news, food processing, frozen and chilled food, fresh produce etc. Remember, the target publications are trade journals not consumer-oriented magazines such as *The Good Food Guide*.

Eventually, having exhausted every search term you should end up with a list of trade titles. This will vary from country to country, although the UK and the US should yield the most names. Including sector related publications this could end up in the UK comprising a list of around 100 publications, in Australia this is likely to be no more than ten.

If you are expanding and on the lookout for new recruits it might also be worthwhile adding any local and/or regional newspapers to the circulation list, as the local media are always looking for good local business stories and the editor will normally cover a story if the product or service creates more jobs or brings some other benefits to the community. In addition, it may help with your recruitment by attracting some speculative CVs.

Enter the details into a consistent spreadsheet format, as a minimum include the trade title, editor's name, email address and phone number. We'll come back to sending out the editorial shortly.

To support the editorial ideally a good sharp photograph is needed, this can also be used in the subsequent e-newsletters, Twitter, Facebook, on your website and to even support the lead generation campaign.

It is said that one picture is worth a thousand words. This point was not missed by another PR master, Napoleon Bonaparte, who is attributed with saying: "Un bon croquis vaut mieux qu'un long discours," or "A good sketch is better than a long speech."

Note the words good sketch, this means that the picture

needs to be sharp and in focus, preferably high resolution, typically around 2 MB, and if it is a hardware product make sure it is taken without any factory clutter such as sweeping brushes, spanners, food waste or bins surrounding it. As a starting point please ask the customer whether it is possible to take a picture. Some customers are more accommodating than others but if you don't ask, the customer can't help. If you need to outsource a photographer, check their portfolio of images, if it is just a set of wedding images try another, as photographing machinery is very different from people. This is because factory machinery is often steel which can be notorious for reflecting the light, the site may not be that well-lit and the expanse to photograph can be daunting.

Depending on relevance, the photographer should have some shielding to put behind any newly supplied equipment to remove background clutter. Subject to the factory manager agreeing, your photographer may also want to apply baby oil or similar to any stainless steel machinery that is to be photographed because the oil stops light reflection and therefore you are more likely to get a decent image.

If you are taking the picture yourself try and photograph just a part of the machine, such as a control panel or the customer's goods being produced using the equipment. If you are a service provider, take a shot of the outside of the factory showing, if possible, signage. It goes without saying that images need to be in focus, if you are not that brilliant with a camera use the automatic settings. Always take lots of pictures preferably from different angles, you can always disregard the ones you don't want but you can't subsequently generate the pictures you didn't take!

Remember the pictures taken will be needed for the editorial, newsletter, social media and possibly even for a leaflet.

At this stage we should now have a PR database in spreadsheet format, some agreed editorial text and some supporting images.

In the next chapter, we'll pull everything together and get the editorial circulated.

Key points and actions you need to take from this chapter

1 - B2B media related PR plays an important role in integrated marketing

2 - Understand the difference between press releases, case studies and features

3 - Always remember that the purpose of the case study is to inform potential customers about the great job you have done for your current customer – through the customer's own words

4 - Take a note of the interview questions and customize them as necessary to your own business

5 - Creating a media database is critical - note the different options

6 - Support the PR with some good photographic images

Chapter 14

How to manage a PR media database and editors to get good publicity

Using a database to store and contact journalists will help automate the distribution of PR material and allow the time for other integrated marketing. Once written, PR material can be used across multiple marketing channels to leverage the maximum return on investment.

According to Czech writer Milan Kundera, business has only two functions - marketing and innovation.

No matter how good your product or service is, if nobody has heard about it then it will fail. Spreading the message requires data, media targets and potential customers. Managing this data and keeping it updated and safe is a key backroom task of any marketing, which includes looking after a separate PR media database.

Managing a PR database well is a never-ending task because editorial staff at the more junior levels are constantly changing, which means the database needs regularly updating.

As a starting point contacts can be compiled into a spreadsheet and then subsequently imported into Outlook as Contact Groups, which were formerly named Distribution Lists. If you are not using Outlook see what options your email program permits.

Outlook allows the multiple circulation of editorial, a message sent to a Contact Group goes to all recipients that are listed in the group which is at zero cost, providing of course you are already using Outlook.

Using Outlook for distribution provides minimal control and there are more sophisticated ways of dealing with editorial contacts which can provide a more bespoke editorial distribution.

If you are using one of the specialist database providers like PRmax (see the previous chapter) you can store them within the cloud based package and even use their distribution service. The alternatives are to store the contacts in a content management system such as ACT!, Salesforce which does email mail merge; or a bespoke package such as Prezly or Media Magnet which will also provide a limited number of incorporated media contact features.

As part of the integrated marketing plan I am strongly recommending that you issue one case study or press release a month. This is because the backbone of the media contacts will be monthly publications whether digital or print. The publications are also unlikely to feature your business more than once per month unless you have got some strong editorial stories.

For many smaller firms even circulating editorial once a month could be a challenge and therefore unless your firm has a PR department or agency on-board, it is always better to complete one decent piece of editorial a month rather than rushing two and then failing miserably to get them published.

Depending on the database route chosen, distribute the PR to the relevant editorial contacts and also don't forget to also send an attached or downloadable digital image to support the story.

Digital publishing publications will be the first to run the editorial story followed by any local media and then subsequently the monthly printed publications.

Clients sometimes ask which is the best type of trade magazine to appear in, digital or print? My advice is both, because some digital magazines have bigger readerships than some print magazines and are also great for search engine optimization.

Conversely, traditional print magazines provide a prestige presentation of your story and can look fantastic at meetings when you pull the publication out of a briefcase and/or it is placed on a reception desk.

In terms of timescale if your editorial has legs, expect some media coverage within a matter of days from circulating the editorial followed by further coverage spanning possibly a few months. Occasionally for reasons sometimes unknown a piece of editorial gets virtually no coverage. Don't get angry if this happens to you but do review the quality of the text submitted and also the number of publications you sent it to. Contrary to popular belief B2B editorial normally fails to get publicity not because of the writing quality (although this can be a contributory reason) but because there is dearth of publications relevant to the story.

Over the course of my business career I have met thousands of editors, deputy editors, feature writers, news editors and journalists. Most of these people have one thing in common, whether they work for television news, a trade title or a local paper and that is a great news story (preferably exclusive) that is relevant to their publications. Don't worry too much about the exclusivity of the story with one trade title because you'll antagonize the rest of your media hit list. Do however, time permitting, phone some of the key trade titles and introduce yourself to the editor or if it is a big publication a relevant journalist, and follow this up with an email containing your contact details. Do also advise your chosen editorial contact (if you want to) that you'd love to give a comment on any future trade news stories and do make available a contact number and email address where the editorial staff can quickly contact you.

It is tempting to follow up a submitted news story that hasn't appeared with a phone call. Most editorial staff are resistant to this process because they have limited time to turnaround their publication without getting tied down with administration type phone calls. Therefore the best follow-up process is normally to send an email. It is useful to get the occasional feedback especially if you have had two or three stories that haven't been published and therefore a phone call wouldn't be unwarranted to a small number of publications that aren't covering your editorial on the pretext of getting some feedback.

If you are following up by phone please don't pick an argument with the editorial staff on the basis you thought it was a good story, what you think is not important, what the editorial team think is paramount. Therefore, if your story hasn't appeared and the publication is giving you some constructive feedback, take it on the chin and don't complain. The publication thereafter will be more supportive of your efforts and if you take on-board some of their recommendations it will be far more supportive of your efforts.

Keeping track of editorial coverage is a challenge because it is unlikely that you'll be able to get a copy of each of the trade publications involved and I wouldn't recommend you set up a media cutting service unless you have a decent media budget due to the costs.

However, I would recommend as a starting point that you establish a Google alert that contains just the name of your firm or part of the name. This will provide a daily update on digital editorial coverage and should pick up some publicity that otherwise would have been missed.

Managing the PR procedure may sound a bit daunting but in all fairness it is just a process and once you have done it a few times it should become second nature. If it makes you feel better even seasoned PR professionals can sometimes struggle to get every PR piece published, so if things don't go smoothly for the first two case studies, don't worry you are not alone.

I'd like to explain the fundamental driver of news and it is a semi-subconscious feature that is embedded in the human brain called storytelling – everyone likes a great story which is one of the reasons that places like Ireland can sometimes punch above its nation's weight.

Telling a great story is a very effective way of developing customer relationships. This old- fashioned idea unites people from all walks of society together and keeps them engaged. A great story transcends continents and even funding.

A great story, product and vision can give a loud voice to even a tiny business start-up. Thirty years ago Hoover vacuum cleaners dominated the UK domestic market. Then a chap called James Dyson came along with a new, better designed vacuum cleaner and told everyone who would listen why his bagless solution using centrifugal force was better. Today Dyson sells in 65 countries, employs 1,000 engineers and is the UK's market leader in vacuum cleaners. According to Euromonitor International in 2014 the Hoover Candy Group now has just 7% of the market. There is no doubt that the combined efforts of a great story and great products have helped Dyson to overtake its rivals.

As the Dyson story illustrates a good story can give a large voice to the new kid on the block, which is why your business needs to craft its own story. This story should not be dishonest but it should be developed around your USP (unique selling proposition), be joined up and explain why your service or product is superior.

According to Tiffani Jones Brown, Content Strategy Lead at Pinterest via Contently: good writing and content strategy makes products, and the marketing of those products, much better. When we do our jobs well, the things we launch are easier and more fun to use. We've seen how changing copy can positively impact sign-ups, engagement and sentiment.

Marketing and storytelling often go hand-in-hand. To capture the attention of an audience you need a good story and the better that story the more attention your product or service will receive. When we hear a good story, our brain acts as if we're feeling and sometimes actually seeing the story.

Many would-be suppliers bombard potential B2B customers

with irrelevant information to the point of boredom. To make a product or service stand out the supplier needs a non-fluffy credible story.

A good story makes our brains behave differently and influences the way humans behave.

Whether you are religious or agnostic books like the bible have through storytelling been influencing the conduct of humans for thousands of years. As an example, take the Old Testament, many of its stories certainly reflect the values and priorities of the culture at the time it was drafted.[1] These values have been embedded into powerful tales that invite the reader or listener to draw their own conclusions.

When Eve ignored her alleged instructions from God and ate the fruit from the Garden of Eden's tree of knowledge, according to the bible she was punished. This is a powerful warning of the doom that could await anyone who ignores a divine order. Noah, who carried out God's instructions to build the ark, survived whilst presumably his neighbors were all drowned.

Not that many years ago a published case study was likely to be the wording you read wrapping around your fish and chips container just a couple of days later. Today getting some initial publicity is just the start of the marketing process. This is because the need for marketing material to plug digital holes and especially case study material has never been greater.

Therefore, press releases, case studies and features can be posted on the website, but not too quickly to ensure that the media can use them first. In addition, all written content can be used in newsletters and as hyperlinks on social media following digital publicity. Also, case studies can be turned into PDF literature for sending to other relevant customers.

At this stage it is possibly time for a word to the wise. Please don't feel overwhelmed by the volume of practical information I have so far shared. Your first integrated marketing campaign probably won't be your best but it will be the beginning of your journey.

As Winston Churchill said after Britain's first battle victory against Germany: "Now this is not the end. It is not even the beginning of the end. But it is, perhaps, the end of the beginning."

Key points and actions you need to take from this chapter

1 - Identify a database or PR database provider for distributing PR material

2 - Work out a writing schedule for what editorial you want to issue each month, typically one per month based on the frequency of the trade titles

3 - Try and cultivate a professional relationship with editors but never ever upset them

4 - Use Google alerts to keep track of editorial coverage

5 - Press releases, case studies and features can be posted on the website, used in newsletters on social media and case studies can be turned into PDF literature

1 The Power of Story by Elizabeth Svoboda, Aeon Media Pty Ltd. 2016

Chapter 15

Photographs: a good image is worth a thousand words

For integrated marketing the use of photography to support media and marketing activities and a consistent? quality house image across the website, social media, print and digital literature and, if applicable, company signage is vital. It tells your audiences that you are professional about what you do and have (hopefully) a recognizable image as part of your company's branding.

According to Elliott Erwitt: "The whole point of taking pictures is so that you don't have to explain things with words." However, that's just for starters because Dr Marshall McLuhan and his son Dr Eric McLuhan, both renowned authorities on communications and media, developed the academic theory that people think in either words or pictures.

The pair also undertook left and right brain research and discovered that right-brained people tend to think more in images and left-brain dominated people will tend to think more in words. According to Roger HB Davies, whose business *Think on Your Feet* provides communication courses, a whole-brain approach is needed for good communication.

As an experienced marketeer I would advocate that good quality photography is an integral part of integrated marketing because part of your target audience will view what you do through images. This doesn't mean that you have to employ a professional photographer for every image your business needs because an android phone and iPhone can take very good pictures unless lighting is an issue. Indeed, the smart phone has made a lot of the old snap happies redundant, although for more formal pictures and those involving images of machinery those old timers still know a few clever tricks, which I am happy to share later in this chapter.

The photographic requirements of integrated marketing splits into the following:

Application	Size	Format	Pixels	Notes
Facebook Business Page Profile Picture	less than 100 KB	RGB JPG file. Images with a logo or text, as a PNG file	180 x 180 pixels	Facebook will resize images
Twitter Profile picture	Maximum 2 MB	JPG, GIF, PNG	400 x 400 pixels	Square image recommended
LinkedIn Company cover image	4MB	JPG, GIF, PNG	1536 x 768 pixels	This image appears larger than the personal
YouTube profile picture		JPG, GIF, BMP or PNG	800 x 800 pixels	
Digital newsletters	Below 100 KB to avoid spam filters	JPG, PNG, GIF	Between 550 to 600 pixels and a length which best fits the content	Typically, 72dpi maximum
Websites	Less than 500 KB	JPG, PNG, GIF	Between 1500 and 2500 pixels wide	Avoid too lower pixels as the image will be blurred
Media to support editorial	2MB	JPG or TIFF	300 dpi	A landscape and portrait shape should be provided
Special applications like branding material	Up to 50MB	EPS, TIFF or JPG	300 dpi	The standard is 300 dpi, but some design houses can handle up to 1200 dpi

Let's start with the basics, for media purposes a colorful, eye-catching photo will enhance the editorial and can increase its chance of getting published. Images should be at least 300dpi

– and at a usable size for publication. It is important to think about photography early on in the process as many pieces of editorial are often delayed when no photo is available and it is easy to miss deadlines waiting for someone to take that all important image.

For pack shots, machinery and other tangible but static awkward items should be taken using studio lighting, which for many businesses means outsourcing.

If you are taking photographs onsite say of machinery at a customer installation it is important that if it's been agreed that the customer will get to see photos before they are used, that this happens. Customers can be very picky and it is therefore vital that if a customer doesn't want certain images used that these are deleted from the files so there is no possibility of them being used by mistake in the future. Any information relating to use of photography should be recorded clearly. If you think a photograph is not suitable for use with editorial you should discuss this with the customer and encourage them to look at other picture options. Remember, at best editors won't use a poor image – and at worst they will!

When taking pictures you need to think a little creatively, a couple of middle-aged men shaking hands won't set the trade media on fire, but the same two men using diagnostic equipment, studying the small print of a contract, using a piece of machinery or browsing a relevant brochure at least creates a picture in tune with what's happening.

This is my first top tip: if you are taking pictures of people, just remember that the face creates shading which can result in underwhelming images that make individuals look a bit odd. To avoid this use flash on your phone or camera even if it is a bright day. Secondly never take a photograph with the subject directly looking towards the sunlight, your subject will squint (or pass out), so it is better to take at a 45-degree angle to the sun. The second top tip is to take as many pictures as possible from different angles, much better to have lots of images to choose from rather than having to take the same picture again.

It should be remembered that photography is two dimensional, this means that people can blend into the background and create a picture that looks likes the person's head has been fused into a piece of machinery. On one occasion I had a client send me some pictures they had taken of their retiring chief executive. The chief executive had chosen to have his picture taken in front of a grandfather clock, however when I looked at the pictures, I discovered that his head was imprinted in substitution for the clock face, sadly we rejected all the images and sent our own photographer to retake them!

There are some people who never smile no matter how hard you or a photographer tries, this can be very frustrating and can result in some very dour pictures. If you can't get the person to smile ask them to blow a raspberry, although it sounds odd the relaxing of the mouth afterwards always creates a natural smile.

Proportionality might seem a strange word to use but if you are taking people pictures with an office or factory in the background to showcase signage, it is important that the building doesn't eclipse the subjects. To address this, get your people to stand a few meters away from the building and take the shot close to them. You may need to play around a little but you will then get some proportionality.

One of the ways to avoid dull pictures is to feature company uniforms, or other colorful work wear, my only advice and it's a personal preference, just avoid creating a sea of brown which can make for a very dull image.

So far, I have talked about people and not equipment. But let's suppose you are marketing some kind of machinery and it is typically made out of aluminum or stainless steel. Taking pictures of silver colored metal if unpainted is hopeless because the light from any flash or artificial background lighting (recommended) will not allow a sharp and representative image to be taken. To address this wipe the machinery in baby oil or olive oil, the oil will absorb light and allow a much better picture to be taken.

If you are involved in taking pictures at your customer's premises it is really important that any background debris is removed and everything looks spick and spam. This means having a tidy up before the picture-taking including removing any background things like offending calendars, leaked oil, discarded food, mouse traps, brooms and any other image spoilers.

Some years ago, I sent a photographer to a well-known manufacturer of airline foods, the customer had been told in advance to prepare for the visit and was given detailed guidance on what was acceptable. When I took a look at the images afterwards, I was horrified, the floor had a dirty shovel on it and a mucky looking hosepipe that was dispensing baked beans onto a very soiled floor. When I took the photographer to task, he responded by saying but you should have seen the place before they had the clean-up!

In service industries like insurance there is a need to be creative as displaying an insurance certificate is not going to have the same impact as a shiny machine or piece of engineering. Look to see how you can link the service to the customer's business. This could include showing the customer holding an insurance certificate on the shop floor with machinery or people all working around the customer.

Key points and actions you need to take from this chapter

1 - Photography should be part of your branding - make sure the website home page image, social media profile images and literature all feature an iconic quality picture that is consistent across all marketing

2 - Decide what size images you need and make sure everything is resized accordingly

3 - Be creative with your photography and take lots of pictures at different angles

4 - The human face creates shadows so use flash to brighten faces

5 - Photography is two dimensional so make sure nothing is behind your subject which is going to distract from the image you want

6 - If you are taking installation pictures to support PR and social media activities always do some pre-preparation work

Chapter 16

Film it - the value of digital footage and how YouTube can add value

To do it properly and in keeping with integrated marketing any footage needs to be presented on YouTube, your company's website, Facebook, Twitter links tweeted and of course hyperlinked on LinkedIn. But that's just for starters because the footage can also be used for sales purposes, shown on a screen at exhibitions and played incessantly in your company's reception area. As the Americans love to say "get more bang for your buck" or as people in my native Yorkshire say "get your money's worth."

Gary Vaynerchuk, New York Times bestselling author, speaker, and internet personality says: "No matter what you do, your job is to tell your story." Vaynerchuk is absolutely right and video content is an important channel for conveying that story.

B2B readers of this book will have mastered if you have reached this far the importance of an integrated marketing approach, although may be puzzled about what to film. So, before we go delving into recording technologies let's look at what is worth recording and more importantly what is likely to give you a return on investment.

Digital footage fits into a number of overlapping camps or to coin a phrase is marketing fluid. Traditionally, larger companies had a pre-scripted corporate video with a voiceover - usually a man with a fancy accent. Depending on what part of the world you are based the voiceover could vary from a posh English public-school to an Adelaide or Boston accent. Thankfully those days are long gone and some kind of ordinary accent should now be used.

The aim of the corporate marketing video (not to be confused with training videos), which has changed little over the years apart from improved quality and graphics thanks to technology, is to promote your company's product or service, showcase your brand, market your whole business and create a feel-good factor to exude confidence and win over potential customers.

Most videos will cover different aspects of your business such as administration, key markets maybe with the help of some graphics, key employees, if relevant production, distribution, vehicles, past milestones and future plans.

It is normal practice to work out the contents of the video and for best results to use a voiceover with short snappy interviews with key members of staff. To produce a video with this level of sophistication generally needs some detailed planning and the help of an external filming company or freelance film maker.

The corporate marketing video still has an important role to play on websites, exhibition stands and of course showing it to prospective customers. The knack is to upload the video to YouTube after approval so that it can be hyperlinked on everything from Facebook to digital mailer pieces, which will allow it to always play properly no matter what the platform and the device the person is using to view it. If you are uploading it to YouTube just remember to disable the adverts, otherwise you could end up promoting somebody else's products!

Whilst your interest in your own business especially if you are the founder will be massive, making a corporate video beyond three minutes will be a massive turn off for your potential audience. So, aim at the outset for two minutes but not more than three.

To augment the corporate marketing video, smaller videos can be produced by you or your marketing team.

These need to be thought through in advance because the same rules apply as per still photography in terms of not picking up any background rubbish, as highlighted in the last chapter.

Most marketing people film using smaller handheld devices such as an iPhone or a separate small video camera. Whilst this is acceptable just be mindful that if you are prone to handshaking or movement it might be worth investing in a small video camera and tripod. The types of footage you can easily film might include a machine in operation, an interview with a key person, some exhibition footage or some other short and simple footage. If you are filming a machine in operation consider adding some music (check for licensing) that will enhance the presentation.

So far so good, therefore the million-dollar question is what kind of return on investment will I get from any of my video footage?

Well from YouTube we can see sometimes bluntly if the figures are disappointing regarding the number of views, however a better call to action and measure is needed. This can be achieved by placing the corporate or brand video on the homepage of your website. New business enquiries should be prompted as to whether they saw the video and did it encourage them to contact you. But the question you should them ask yourself is on average how much is a new customer worth to your company, in effect what's their value?

One of the things that video footage is good at presenting, although not always accurately, is the culture of a business. Do the people look like us, are they friendly, would they be fun or boring to trade with, does the firm look prosperous or down at heel, does the firm look small but professional, large but impersonal? The type of culture in a business really matters to some people and in preparation for filming I would strongly advise you to consult some of your satisfied customers to get an understanding of why they trade with your firm. Once you have this information it becomes much easier to reflect it in the format of the video.

When interviewing, bear in mind that most people including

senior members of staff are not naturals when it comes to speaking to the camera, so it it's always best to try and script them in advance providing that it doesn't look too stilted.

When you are recording, always get people to look straight into the camera, which might sound strange but they will be repaid by looking confident and knowledgeable. For complicated presentations there is the dv prompter app on the Apple Store which allows a script to be slowly presented on an iPad that can be held by a third party next to the camera. This autocue saves a lot of hassle and if you have something serious to talk about such as the sale of a business, bereavement etc., it can help with presenting a more formal presentation.

As with all marketing, you need to think about the key messages in advance of filming and what you want to include and who or what you don't want to include! All the key messages should be in tune with your integrated marketing campaign, this means having footage that you can use over multiple platforms and content that encourages people from other businesses to engage with you.

External support is available from a variety of sources ranging from freelance camera people who will do a good recording but will need you to do the storyboard and script, to filming companies who will do everything for you based on an initial briefing. From my own experience for bigger projects the help of a freelance or camera crew for corporate videos is invaluable.

However, no matter how much you pay you will still need to do your homework. A few years ago, I was involved in supporting the launch of a new learning facility for the fish industry, my job was to handle the PR part, and others were employed to film the launch. After various impressive speeches and calls to action including music and show dancing, the director of ceremonies said we'll now switch to the Mayor who will eat a fish which had earlier been cooked by a household name chef. In the control room the producer said: "switch to camera, 1, 2 and 3 and action." The three cameras tuned into the Mayor who was subsequently fed a piece of white fish by the highly expensive celebrity chief. The glitzy compère who had rushed down the stairs to meet the tight itinerary said in a rather flowery voice: "...and what do you think to that Mr Mayor?" and the Mayor replied in a very flat northern voice: "I don't like it!"

Despite all the so-called preparations nobody had asked him if he liked fish. My advice is leave nothing to chance, plan, plan and plan some more.

Key points and actions you need to take from this chapter

1 - Decide what type of footage you need and where this fits into your integrated marketing plan

2 - If you are new to filming start with a corporate video to present your culture and other USPs

3 - Consider making short video clips of machinery or services in-house using a smartphone of professional recording camera

4 - Always plan in advance what you need and prepare a storyboard even if you are using an external agency to support you

5 - Make sure that all footage that is produced is used across all your company's marketing platforms from social media to the website and digital mailers

Social media, the importance of using relevant B2B platforms and how to automate it

Like it or hate it, social media is an important part of the integrated marketing toolkit, yet the tools that are jointly called "social media" significantly vary between the different platforms. For integrated marketing purposes social media allows earlier marketing activities to be promoted or amplified to significantly extend their reach, which adds value to any campaign.

"The first rule of social media is that everything changes all the time. What won't change is the community's desire to network," says Kami Huyse, digital strategist, speaker and author.

There is an odd age thing between different marketeers: most people under 30 don't understand why every business doesn't have social media accounts and many over 50 think it's a pointless method of engaging with potential customers. Both groups miss the important point, that social media is also a great SEO tool and with proper research and a strategy, certain social media platforms can generate sales leads and even sales.

Marketing preferences and platform features are now changing frequently, which makes developing and implementing B2B social media strategies fluid and at times challenging.

According to Influencer Marketing[1] there are now 50+ social media sites, however most of these should be discounted for B2B marketing because their demographics don't match the audiences we need to reach with our integrated marketing campaign. As an example, why would you target businesses on Snapchat when it is primarily aimed at children and teenagers and provides a simple way for them to share everyday moments while simultaneously making them look great.

My recommended social media platforms for B2B integrated marketing are, at the time of publication, the following:

LinkedIn - this business-driven platform has one of the most impressive demographics of any network. LinkedIn has over half a billion people[2] connected to its platform and has a clear business focus. According to Microsoft's own figures 23% of registered users use LinkedIn monthly and, anecdotally, engagement and interaction tend to be driven by a small group of power users and job seekers. Compounding this for brands is an algorithm that defaults to displaying top posts in the LinkedIn feed, and some ambiguity about notifications and display to your organic network.

Company profiles are linked to a personal account, but company profiles differ slightly because they don't allow one-to-one InMail communication. So paid options should be considered to enhance corporate content on LinkedIn; we'll cover this in more detail in the next chapter.

All businesses should start by setting up a corporate page on LinkedIn and then posting relevant corporate information and information about your product or service on a weekly or at worst case, monthly basis. This information needs to be informative - perhaps built around a recent sale or contract - with some kind of call to action.

Facebook - most research on Facebook page reach has arrived at the same conclusion: reach has been declining for a number of years.[3] Some of these studies look at the relative number of views per post, while others project views as low as 1%.

The consensus is that brand ability to reach Facebook fans is slowly diminishing with time. However, Facebook is the most popular social media network and is way ahead of the rest, so with more social media networks coming online, it could be that the market is just becoming, like television, more fragmented.

A recent anomaly in the data has been a reported consistency or increase in reach for video posts.

This is ultimately where Facebook sees its future and something your business should embrace.

However, Facebook has lots going for it such as the ability to cheaply boost posts by paying a small advertising fee, the opportunity to advertise based on a particular job, location or age or all of them and lots of other parameters, please see next chapter. It is also worth remembering that Facebook is there to complement your website with content because customers and friends of your business will visit your Facebook page to find out what's happening within your company, see content such as pictures, read your latest news and/or explore forthcoming events.

The reach of **Twitter** is also difficult to measure but is also relatively low.[4] A lot of companies claim to have accurate data on reach, and so does Twitter (although they calculate reach as the number of followers who saw a post if they were on Twitter at the time, rather than a true measure of reach to overall followers). Twitter now has an algorithm that likely further skews that impression and engagement rate.

Twitter is more action-paced, compact and is a quicker way to communicate with your audience. In a nutshell Twitter is a lake of information based on a maximum 280-character content waiting to be explored by reading, clicking, following and hopefully re-tweeting to expand the reach of your message.

The United States President's success using Twitter as a communications platform perhaps skews people's perception of Twitter's reach. It is important to understand that most of the awareness of the President's Tweets come from press coverage of the Tweets rather than from Twitter itself. This is an organic amplification mechanism that cannot be emulated by a business or even many brands. On the other hand, proactive

Direct Messaging is an option for Twitter (with read receipts). However, there is evidence suggesting that many people don't read their DMs because they tend to attract spam. That said, at least one academic paper demonstrates that DMs are more useful to generate conversion events than public Twitter. The challenge for your business is that the technology is currently not in place to direct message a lot of Twitter people at the same time, but you can at least tweet information, which has to be the easiest and cheapest digital mailshot ever.

In the commercial arena **YouTube** and the likes of Vimeo and Spotify are video sharing services where users can watch, like, share, comment on and upload their own videos. These video services can be accessed on PCs, laptops, tablets and via mobile phones. The majority of users on YouTube are either visitors who have not logged into their accounts or are not even members in the first place. Most YouTube users are between the ages of 16 and 24.

In the commercial arena YouTube is popular with firms and organizations that wish to upload event or product footage, as the videos can be hyperlinked into other digital content such as websites, tweets, Facebook and blogs.

Social media also plays an important role because not only is the number of Twitter followers and Facebook likes, network connections on LinkedIn and views on YouTube used by Google as one of the factors to determine your website's ranking, social media also allows you to increase your media research for PR stories as well as allowing your business to publish content for free.

There are of course lots of other social media channels but for the purpose of integrated B2B marketing I have ignored the others as most are not relevant.

A significant amount of time can be wasted on social media with often a poor B2B level of engagement. For this reason, some technology is needed to control the frequency of posting and which also lets you post on more than one social media platform at a time.

There are a number of automated social media packages that can do this, the most popular are Hootsuite, Buffer, Sprout Social and Loomly.

For the purposes of this book I am recommending Hootsuite, because it offers a cut down version of the package for free and because it integrates with a large number of social channels including the four channels highlighted as most relevant for business in this chapter: Twitter, Facebook, YouTube and LinkedIn. The four channels are an integral part of integrated marketing which is what this book is about.

Use Hootsuite to schedule the posting of content based on press releases, case study content, editorial published, content on your website, nubs of news and other information not just about your business but the sector in general, that is likely to be relevant to your core audience. The great thing about Hootsuite is that it allows posts to be scheduled and created over all the different platforms outlined. This means that you don't need to spend ages on social media each day, you can put posts together at the beginning of the month and then sit back and watch them appear each week, or if you have enough material even each week day.

One of the most important reasons for using social media is to increase the outreach of existing material. So, if a case study that appeared in a digital magazine reaches a further 1,000 relevant contacts, that's a result. Since Google is also over the platforms as part of its ranking process it is important to have all of the social media platforms linked to your website's home page and if you plan to post daily, which I accept is ambitious for B2B, you should also have on the home page live Twitter, Facebook, LinkedIn and YouTube links.

The hardest issue with social media is getting to the level of followers, likes and views that gives you sufficient leverage to make an impact. To get to the required level of engagement with potential customers requires some mind-numbing work.

To find potential Twitter followers, look at the followers of relevant trade publications, competitors and companies that you are already trading with. Twitter allows you to follow up to 5,000 people, however once you reach this threshold Twitter imposes some restrictions based on the ratio of the number of people you follow to the number of people who follow you. Therefore, you will need a proactive approach to dumping people who don't follow you back.

An interesting feature about Twitter and Facebook is the ability to hashtag content. The hashtag should contain only one word without spaces, so no punctuation can be included. The hashtag should be included within or after your message, eg #PhilipAllott. However, only use hashtags sparingly, when they add value to your product or service.

Both platforms allow video content and Facebook has announced that it expects a significant proportion of future posts to be video related, effectively providing a hybrid version of YouTube.

In a selective news age era, many people are searching Facebook and especially Twitter for the latest news; adding a hashtag allows people to find you when they search for that content and it also allows Facebook and Twitter the opportunity to send you a direct message when people have hashtagged your name.

Twitter is faster than Google at indexing news content and it is therefore often the preferred news source for journalists and media outlets following breaking news stories.

For business purposes a Facebook corporate page will need setting up, which is managed through a personal account. Administration rights can be given to multiple people with a Facebook account so if necessary, putting content up can be delegated to others, but this should be done to supplement content issued via Hootsuite or one of its rivals, not to replace it. A Facebook business page (or corporate page which is the same) is easy to create. This should comprise the business name and description, the page name should be your business name or another name such as a product that people will search for. You can use the About section to inform people what your business does, it will also need some nice pictures for the profile and cover images. These should present your business in a positive way. Many firms use a combination of a profile picture and logo. For the cover picture, use an image of your premises, products or service.

Finally, link the site to your website and decide what call to action you need, for example clicking to your website and you can even add on Facebook a Call to Action button. The overall aim is for people to like your page and this can be done by asking people to visit the site, tweeting out a link via Twitter and of course hashtagging content.

LinkedIn makes up the trio of word driven platforms and provides a number of useful business features. One of these features is the ability to verify contacts and sometimes even identify contacts using LinkedIn. Where companies have a no names policy but you need to find out, say, the name of a production manager, LinkedIn can be the solution. In addition, because the name has been published on LinkedIn or on any other social media platform it is considered to be in the public domain and therefore using the name (providing you don't break any other laws like the right for erasure) is considered outside the scope of GDPR.

Another of these LinkedIn features is the ability to join existing connections and to expand your product or service customers through word-of-mouth. It's also considered the best social network platform for lead generation. Like all platforms LinkedIn is only as good as the content posted so information must be up to date with a detailed and fully completed Company

Page.

One of the nice features of LinkedIn is the ability to set up special groups dedicated to a particular industry. For B2B niche marketing this will allow you to join these and find individuals engaged in sectors you would like to sell into. InMail communication as highlighted earlier allows personal messages to be sent to other people who are connected with you. Other features include the ability to see who has viewed your personal profile and something called 'Get Introduced.' A lot of businesses consider LinkedIn a useful platform for not only creating website traffic but as a prospecting tool, through the development of thought leadership through the hyperlinking of whitepapers and of course recruiting new staff members.

The key thing to remember with LinkedIn that a lot of the interactive things like InMail come from your own personal account rather than the Company Page. There are also a number of targeted advertising options and I'll highlight these in detail during the next chapter.

YouTube is owned by Google, although don't expect that this automatically places the content on a pedestal above the preceding platforms outlined. Indeed, Google has its own challenges with social media and had to withdraw its platforms Google+ and before that Google Wave and Google Buzz.

It is relatively easy to set up a YouTube business account which can be achieved through a few clicks.

You'll need to complete the About section, provide relevant video content which can be filmed on a smartphone and after uploading should be optimized for your target market.

Hyperlinks from the video content can be posted on Facebook, LinkedIn and tweeted out using Twitter.

YouTube is particularly useful for showing machinery in operation, providing tutorials, past webinar events and for linking video content to your website, digital mailer pieces and hyperlinking to other platforms including third party websites operated by trade associations and exhibition organizers.

The advantage of YouTube is that the footage will always play without the user having to download any special software.

A key point to emphasize is that, due to YouTube's ownership, it has its own set of parameters to optimize the video people may be searching for. Therefore, when a video is uploaded, you will need to provide a title, video description, and tags (like key descriptive words). These are important otherwise the video won't be easily found in YouTube searches, so please don't ignore them.

Like the other platforms there is the opportunity to advertise on YouTube through adverts, which will be covered in the next chapter.

In terms of all four social channels they are high maintenance in the early days with relatively low levels of engagement until you have sufficient relevant content posted and sufficient outreach through connections to have a real impact.

Some method also needs to be put in place to measure social media engagement to see how your different platforms are performing, this is a feature that is available on Hootsuite or Talkwalker. The key point to make is that it is vital that your posted material engages with your audience. For most B2B SMEs this is a problem because you often don't have enough exciting news to turn heads and therefore will need to regurgitate industry news or general information that is relevant to your business and customers. One of the best ways of building engagement is to produce 'how to' videos on YouTube that you then promote via Facebook, Twitter and LinkedIn - and of course your own website.

The good thing about social media is that it extends the reach of your business in a way that is difficult to achieve by other marketing methods, but do remember that it is not a substitute for the other integrated marketing actions outlined in this book. In terms of payback expect increased name awareness, enhanced reputation and some sales enquires, although not in vast numbers because your offering is B2B - and lastly further SEO for your website.

Key points and actions you need to take from this chapter

1 - Facebook, Twitter, LinkedIn and YouTube are key integrated marketing components

2 - Set up accounts with each of the four and where applicable business or corporate pages

3 - Use Hootsuite for automated posting as it will allow you to plan content many weeks in advance and post across all networks

4 - Make sure that you invest time in building engagement from soliciting likes, followers and YouTube video views

5 - Social media helps with SEO work so make sure the four platforms outlined are linked to your website

1 https://influencermarketinghub.com/social-media-sites

2 As of May 2020, LinkedIn stated it had 675 million+ members

3 BuzzSumo

4 https://venturebeat.com/2018/10/25/twitter-loses-9-million-monthly-active-users-in-q3-2018-its-steepest-decline-ever/

Chapter 18

Digital advertising, why it often fails and how it can work

Digital advertising is ideal for supporting integrated marketing. It should be noted that advertising is not a silver bullet and for best results should always be used to augment other promotional activities rather than as a standalone solution.

Digital advertising covers a vast array of platforms and the aim of this chapter is to cover the most relevant B2B outlets and to provide an element of context in how they fit into an integrated marketing strategy. The subsequent chapter covers traditional adverting in print and digital trade publications.

To quote Jeff Bezos: "It's hard to find things that won't sell online." However, in Bezos' case he has his own platform, Amazon, but for your business we need to find some.

At the top of most people's digital advertising list is Google Ads (rebranded in 2019 from Google AdWords), which is one of the most effective methods of getting more traffic to your website, producing enquiries and potentially sales.

Google's Ads' competitors include Bing, which incorporates Yahoo, the social media channels and even in some circumstances, television advertising. Most of the social media channels are not relevant to B2B advertising because they are unable to easily reach the target markets for your business, however I'll explore shortly those that are appropriate for your business.

To put the relevance of B2B advertising into some kind of context, the size of the market to sell your products or service is limited by the number of businesses within the sector and therefore the smaller the potential customer base, the lower the effectiveness of any advertising campaign. One way to test this is to look on Google Ads at the number of people searching on a particular word or phrase, if it is below 200 a month then it is niche and if it is below 50 it is very niche.

For all advertising platforms the lower the potential outcome the greater the cost of each sale. Let's say the cost of advertising is $1,000per month and you make $10,000 profit on the sale of, say, each food processing machine, that's $9,000 profit. But if your business generates only 10 sales leads over six months and it only converts three of these into sales, the cost of the campaign will have been $6,000 less the gross profit of $30,000 = $24,000 net of advertising costs. At this level of return it is still worth trialing an advertising campaign.

Conversely, if you are selling a service such as insurance and you only make a profit of $1,000 per sale, unless you can generate and convert more than one lead a month, your campaign is at break-even and after taking into account overheads for servicing the work, all sales leads are loss making. To understand more about the size of the potential markets you want to reach, please revisit chapter three.

If you were to start with just one platform it should start with Google Ads because as we know from earlier chapters Google is the dominant search engine and handles the majority of the 3.5 billion searches undertaken each day[1] but and there is always a but, its method of advertising unless you are using its subsidiary YouTube, is all text driven, which can get lost on a younger decision making audience.

The big selling point with Google (and Bing) Ads is that advertising can also help kickstart a new website and generate traffic whilst the organic search terms get optimized and settle down. In addition, Ads can be used to supplement SEO efforts where a website is limited with the number of key words and phrases it can be customized around.

The practicalities of using Google involve setting up a Google account, attaching a debit or credit card, agreeing a monthly budget and the most important factor of all researching the search terms which are the most relevant and any additional search terms suggested by Google. The last bit involves setting some goals, this could be as simple as choosing a goal that corresponds to the main thing that you want your campaign to achieve for your business. As an example, if you would like to monitor people who after viewing your ads visit your website, you can select 'Website traffic' as the goal.

Bing is owned by Microsoft and works like Google on a pay per click (PPC) basis. Advertising on Bing gets your advert onto three search engines: Bing, Yahoo and AOL plus various other partner sites.

Google and Bing both allow up to 80 characters in one longer description field. Where Bing wins is that because Yahoo and MSN provide financial reporting, Bing ads tend to have higher CTRs for financial services and things like home shopping, which is perhaps less relevant for B2B.

Bing's demographic research is complementary to Google's, according to instapage.com,[2] Bing allows adverts to reach an older and more educated audience. Instapage says almost 40% of the Bing network ranges from 35 to 54 years old, and nearly three-quarters of Bing users are over the age of 35.

The cost of Bing Ads is much lower than Google and there is a nice option allowing you to import your Google Ads. In terms of creating an account, it is done through a Microsoft account, which after setting up your details prompts for bids and budgets, landing page URLs, tracking templates, Ad extensions and Ads you want to import from Google.

Social media advertising has fragmented some of the markets targeted by Google and Bing because of the vast choice of platforms. Comparing like for like is also difficult because one of the challenges with social media is getting accurate data to support a B2B advertising strategy. All the main providers offer statistics, but there are concerns about the accuracy of the information supplied.

B2B businesses are more likely to be familiar with Google Ads advertising and may have historically discounted social media as a suitable advertising platform. If so, I'd like you to reconsider, because Facebook, LinkedIn, Twitter and YouTube can reach additional B2B markets, for example YouTube has 1.5 billion people logging on each month and Facebook has over 1.55 billion monthly active users. Therefore, if you have an advertising budget, social media involving just Facebook, LinkedIn, Twitter and YouTube should be considered as part of the marketing mix.

Strictly speaking advertising should only be a small part of your integrated marketing campaign because the overall aim is to try and squeeze as much as possible out of each task to support an additional marketing action, as illustrated by the wheel at the start of this book. At the start of integrated marketing, social media advertising can significantly help extend the reach of your promotional activities including creating some website backlinks and also helping to support your social media posts until the platforms have created sufficient organic followers and likes.

This is where Facebook advertising gets interesting because you can set up an advert to appear when the demographics of the user's profile match the job title and employer you wish to target in order to boost a conventional Facebook post. Unlike Google, Facebook and to a lesser extent Twitter and LinkedIn have platforms that involve people publicly sharing details of their lives. On Facebook this includes love and marriage to personal interests, hobbies, careers, beliefs, children and even ideologies including politics.

Whilst Google Ads are very text driven, Facebook, Twitter, YouTube and to a lesser extent LinkedIn can be created as a combination of blended video, images and other visual content in news feeds, allowing your business to take advantage of the more persuasive features that visual ads can provide.

This type of advert can also be conveyed as aspirational messaging enabling them to be far more convincing. The adverts only appear when your advertising criteria is met so in theory the advert should not appear to anyone not meeting the advertising conditions required. The big selling point of social media advertising is that you can not only target by job title, but also age, geography, industry sector. Twitter has a slightly different approach to targeting than Facebook and has advertising options that include keywords, conversation topics, forthcoming events and even behavior.

However, as always it is not quite that simple, as sometimes it is impossible to drill down to the precise industry and/or job titles needed as the fields can be too broad, even on LinkedIn which is all about employment status.

Facebook's massive user base can provide better results than Twitter when combined with the right data combination. Twitter is five times more expensive than Facebook based on the Cost Per Million (CPM). However, comparing the cost between the two can be somewhat challenging as both use bidding, which can vary your cost per click (CPC) tremendously. If you decide to run with Facebook don't forget to install Facebook's Pixel which allows you to track and optimize around campaign goals through the action of visitors visiting certain pages and completing forms.

To reach the right type of B2B companies consideration should also be given to advertising on LinkedIn for new business, if you only have a limited budget this should be directed at LinkedIn and, say, Google Ads, once your Facebook and Twitter accounts have got sufficient organic engagement.

Like the other platforms the setup of LinkedIn allows advertising based on industry, job title, age, geography etc., using a combination of all. However, LinkedIn also allows a number of different options comprising sponsored content, which enables your business to reach out to a larger audience than can be attained organically. Typical adverts are based around text adverts like Facebook and Twitter paid on a CPC basis. These adverts can be linked to your firm's homepage, LinkedIn group pages and profile pages and sponsored InMail. The latter enables your business to send personalized material directly to LinkedIn members' inboxes.

LinkedIn also has a nice feature to retarget people who have recently visited your website. Although slightly fiddly to set up, as you will need to install or have someone install LinkedIn's Insight Tag onto your website, it means that you can retarget the same people with adverts on LinkedIn, which is effectively second chance advertising.

The advertising on LinkedIn works by impressions when your advert appears because it meets the target criteria set or when someone clicks on a url, such as a link to your website.

In niche marketing, where every sales lead has to be nurtured, LinkedIn can be far more lucrative in terms of payback because you only incur a cost when your advert appears to people who have been on your company's website. LinkedIn will also share details about who has clicked on your text adverts. However, this is limited to a breakdown as to the type of individuals clicking. You can view this information online in Campaign Manager or it can be downloaded in a CSV spreadsheet format. This is still useful as it provides a useful guide as to whether you are reaching the right targets.

YouTube is the second most used search engine after Google therefore it should be included as part of your digital marketing strategy.

Although your ad will appear on YouTube, you'll manage your campaign using Google's Ads platform despite your chosen vehicle being a video advert. The platform claims it is easy to set up through a few easy steps to get your video advert up and running. Whilst this may be so, the Google Ads platform is clunky. At the start you'll be prompted to link the advertising campaign for administrative purposes to your own Google account or will be required to set a new one up.

In terms of what your social media adverts should promote, clearly you want to highlight to people your product or service. To do this effectively you might want to offer something a bit eye-catching to engage your chosen audience. This might comprise some kind of warranty, for example at my own marketing agency we offer a publicity guarantee. A lot of B2B advertising is based on brand and supply awareness and driving traffic, all traffic created should be driven to your website rather than your social media pages.

Remember, the only time costs are incurred is when individuals click on the advert and go to your firm's website.

Should you advertise with Google and/or Bing or any of the social media platforms, you'll need to refine and develop your campaign, by testing different wording to see which combination delivers the best results.

Getting the targeting and wording right for B2B advertising is critical as otherwise you'll blow your budget on showing it to students and others who have no interest in buying our fictional food machinery or a service-like insurance. This is one of the reasons most social media advertising campaigns fail, because the majority of advertising money is spent on showing the adverts to people who have no relevance to the product or service you want to sell, and even worse you can end up annoying them.

This might sound slightly odd but if you offer an industrial service applicable to lots of B2B businesses in a certain area, it is now possible to advertise on television. In the UK this is offered by ITV using postcode targeting. The advertising is done through something called TV Hub which is the digital destination for all ITV's channels and online services across mobile, PC, and connected TV. The service has 28.4 million viewers, but by using a small number of postcodes to target it is possible to run a campaign for as little as $2,000 plus the cost of the advert production.

The starting point for any digital advertising campaign is to do some research, look at what each of the platforms can offer to match with the audience you would like to connect with. Are your competitors advertising and if so, which platforms are they using?

Once you have decided which platforms (including Google and Bing) look likely to provide the best return, the campaign needs to focus on the marketing messages you wish to convey. Remember, whilst you may work in a very flat industrial sector, these need to be upbeat and engaging.

The next item on the agenda should be to agree a monthly advertising budget. Companies often ask me what percentage of turnover this should be based on, which is virtually impossible to say as digital advertising is just part of the marketing mix.

However, the Business Development Bank of Canada[3] says a rule of thumb guide is that B2B companies should spend between 2% and 5% of their turnover on marketing. This of course encompasses everything including digital advertising.

With digital advertising there is no one-size-fits-all solution and therefore it is advisable to run a pilot campaign and to step up with the platforms that are providing some effective marketing traction. The last item, as already stated, is to determine your marketing goals and what you would like to measure.

Key points and actions you need to take from this chapter

1 - Learn about the suggested advertising platforms and how they can be harnessed to market B2B products and services

2 - Setup a Google Ads campaign account even if you don't intend to advertise with Google as it will give you access to search term volumes

3   - The recommended advertising platforms from this chapter are Google, Bing, Facebook, LinkedIn, Twitter and YouTube, so consider the type of marketing messages you wish to promote and which of the suggested platforms offer the most likely best return

4   - Determine your marketing messages, what call to action do you want to achieve, for example visit your website and/or make contact?

5   - Put in place methods for measuring your performance

6   - Consider running a pilot campaign

1   https://www.internetlivestats.com/google-search-statistics/

2   https://instapage.com/blog/bing-ads-vs-google-ads

3   https://www.bdc.ca/en/articles-tools/marketing-sales-export/marketing/pages/what-average-marketing-budget-for-small-business.aspx

Chapter 19

When and how to advertise, understanding traditional print and digital magazine campaigns

Few B2B businesses get great results from exclusively advertising, but properly done it is possible to leverage from publishers free editorial, webinars and even guest speaking opportunities, making it a useful integrated marketing cog.

American film producer, Joseph E Levine once said: "You can fool all the people all the time if the advertising is right and the budget is big enough." Levine clearly knew a few things about advertising films because at the time of his passing he had been involved in 497 movies as either a producer, distributor or financier.

In an earlier chapter we spoke about how digital advertising through the bigger search engines and social media platforms can play an important role in conveying your marketing messages in alignment with an integrated marketing campaign. However, so far in this book we haven't actually talked about traditional on-page advertising. It is not that this kind of advertising hasn't got a role to play in helping your business increase its sales, it is simply that it is expensive and therefore for many B2B firms something of a luxury.

That said advertising can be used, funding permitting, for things like supplementing PR campaigns for example through the purchase of space to support an in-depth feature article or some other PR that without advertising support wouldn't appear. Social media and LinkedIn advertising is covered in detail in the last chapter, so this chapter is devoted to traditional advertising whether digital or print in B2B trade magazines.

Trade publication advertising also has a role to play where

there are a very limited number of titles to choose from and therefore editorial coverage of your product or service may be limited, or where you have a small number of topics that you can write about and don't yet have any case studies to submit to the trade media.

To understand how publications generate their advertising revenue is a good start to working out the sort of advertising rates you should be paying, and the likely outcome of running a (supporting) advertising campaign in parallel with your integrated marketing campaign.

Advertising costs are normally calculated by the size of the advert and the numbers of readers that it is circulated to by internet or post. A very simple calculation is to divide the cost of the advert by the number of readers to determine the cost per reader. However, working out the cost per reader is only the start of the process.

As explained in the PR chapter trade titles are either printed, digital or a combination of the two. Advertising in a digital title is nearly always cheaper than the printed version but ironically can be more effective. The reason for this is because digital titles can create backlinks to your website which boost the visibility of your firm's website and therefore the number of enquiries it will deliver, even if the site has a number of shortcomings.

Traditionally in the B2B sector, print publications have ruled supreme and have been able to command within reason whatever advertising rates they have demanded. The UK and Republic of Ireland print and digital publications are split between those that are ABC audited (Audit Bureau of Circulations) and those that have just a publisher's statement.

In the US and Canada the Alliance for Audited Media (AAM), and in Australia the Audited Media Association of Australia (AMAA) are responsible for reporting accurate circulation figures for digital and print magazines to stop over-enthusiastic publishers publishing erroneous numbers.

If you are considering advertising always go with an audited trade title if possible although please do accept that you may pay more for the privilege. This is because there is no way of verifying a publisher's self-announced circulation statement.

Over the years I have seen some horrendous practices where publishers for example have shipped huge numbers of magazines to factories employing large numbers of shop floor workers so that these, most probably disinterested, employees can read the magazines in their leisure time.

Having decided on the appropriate trade titles effort is then needed to determine the best size of the advert and its frequency. Unlike some other promotional activities such as exhibiting at annual trade shows, frequency and a subtle repetition is the key to successful advertising - not necessarily how big the advert is.

Modern advertisers talk about effective frequency, which is the number of times individuals need to be exposed to an advertiser's message before a connection and possibly contact is made and before further exposure is a waste of resources. Effective frequency is still a controversial area and many in the advertising industry have differing views. A typical frequency would be five or six times before the reader starts to connect with the advert and can remember reading it, which is part of the marketing touches as covered in earlier chapters.

If the purpose of the advert is just to generate revenue for the magazine in return for the trade title running your editorial article, then I would suggest that you negotiate the smallest and cheapest advert that the trade title will accept. However, if you have decided that you need a regular advert for the reasons I have already outlined, then consideration needs to be given to developing a series of adverts that tell a story or outline a proposition to the reader over a number of issues. This is because running exactly the same advert five or six times becomes boring and can frustrate readers, so my advice is to find a small design agency and ask them to develop a series of adverts. These are often called storyboards, because they tell a story over a series of adverts.

The size of the advert is not the most critical factor, the most important aspect is the cost per reader and location of the advert within the publication. The best locations are near the jobs section (if there is one), or near the front and preferably on the top right-hand side if it is a print or PDF type publication. Remember your advert will typically be read four times less than editorial and that editorial could be your case study or press release, so your advert really does need to catch the reader's eye.

From my own experience running advertising on its own will yield a poor return so despite what the publisher's sales people will tell you, run your advertising at the same time that your mailer is getting emailed or your company is following up the mailer or in the next edition that follows a piece of editorial you have had published.

Few companies in the B2B sector can afford to run a twelve-month campaign due to prohibitive costs. So the timing of the adverts appearing needs to coincide with the time when companies will most want your product or service. In some B2B industries this is reasonably easy to predict such as very early spring to sell farm machinery, summer for meat packing or early July if you would like a retailer to list your products for Christmas.

However, not all sectors are seasonally sensitive, some following the economic cycle. At the start of the 2008 recession an unusual range of businesses enjoyed an unexpected uptake in sales. This included pizza delivery companies because fewer people could afford to eat out, shoe repair shops because people started to make do and mend, and safe retailers because banking confidence had been eroded. Working out the best areas for product or service demand is the key to successful advertising because most people don't buy umbrellas in the middle of summer and summer shorts (short pants) in December.

In terms of the advert design, try and get a design agency to create something with impact. The advert doesn't need your firm's postal address but it does need your phone number, website and preferably an email address. Many years ago, I worked with computer dealers, one of them insisted on never having any spare white space in adverts despite my howls of protest. Needless to say, his advert became overcrowded and people couldn't read the text and stopped buying his products, not surprisingly he is no longer trading.

Advertising as part of an integrated marketing campaign is what this book is about, however there will be other opportunities to advertise in classified adverts at the back of publications, yellow pages and numerous online and print directories. Some of these adverts can yield a return on investment and if the cost isn't significant, they can be worth a trial. However, the number one place that potential customers will look to find your services is on the internet and therefore the most important investment should be your website headed by an integrated marketing campaign.

Even if you only follow a small amount of the pragmatic guidance advocated by this book, do not try and find a shortcut by spending the majority of your budget on advertising, as there are no shortcuts to generating new business, just great planning, implementation and yes, just a tiny bit of luck. Advertising does indeed have a role to play but the best results will be from using it as part of a wider marketing campaign not as a solo solution.

Key points and actions you need to take from this chapter

1 - Advertising costs are normally calculated by the size of the advert and the number of readers, learn the circulation figures and also whether these are independently verified

2 - Get a design agency to create an advert, or series of adverts,

that create impact

3   - Don't put all your eggs in one basket by spending a fortune on advertising at the expense of the rest of your campaign

4   - Any advertising should be part of an integrated marketing campaign and not standalone. For example, aiming to create website traffic, support social media or editorial collateral

Chapter 20

Permission marketing: what it is and how it can work for your business

Permission marketing may seem at first glance an unusual topic to include in a book on integrated marketing. However, using permission marketing correctly allows sales leads to be generated from social media and other marketing platforms, where hyperlinks can be utilized, thus effectively extending their marketing reach.

It would be amiss in writing a book about integrated marketing if I failed to mention permission marketing. The idea was developed by Seth Godin[1] in the late 1990s and was promoted as the marketing classic for the internet age.

Godin's research found that successful campaigns were those where the customer's consent was obtained. Theories were developed by him around a number of marketing components. Analysts of Godin's work highlight:

- Anticipation: people will anticipate the service/product information from the company.
- Personalization: the marketing information explicitly relates to the customer.
- Relevance: the marketing information is something that the buyer is interested in.

The rather engaging book goes on to talk about turning strangers into friends and friends into customers and is published by Pocket Books.

What many commentators miss is that Godin was an early supporter of integrated marketing. In the book's 'first steps to getting going with permission marketing' he encourages readers to build a series of storyboards that are consistent, which he calls 'communication suites.' These storyboards comprise emails, letters, webpages and phone scripts.

The key point from Godin is that if people have opted in to receive material, they are more likely to engage. Whilst this will work with consumer campaigns it has limited merit with B2B campaigns, where the target audience might be measured in a few thousand as opposed to millions of consumers.

During the run up to the introduction of GDPR in Europe all businesses across the EU were encouraged to update their databases promoting customers and prospects to re-opt-in to continue to receive digital mailing pieces. The average level of both consumer and business contacts re-opting-in was around 5%, so in effect 95% of possibly good quality data was lost.

The failure by many well-known companies to understand GDPR and correctly apply the law must have set their marketing back three or more years. Had they understood GDPR they would have known that there are six lawful ways to process personal data, of which consent is just one and legitimate interest might have been a better choice, subject to certain safeguards, given that no consent is required.

Where permission marketing does have a role to play is in the sharing of information in return for consent to market. This is a relatively simple concept and works along the lines that you send out a social media tweet with a link and/or have a website page link that your prospective customer is encouraged to click. For example, download a report on food machinery, or cost-effective insurance for manufacturing – in keeping with this book's themes. When the contact attempts to download the information they are prompted to enter their email address and phone number, after which they can proceed with the download.

If you decide to do this, it is important that you get the individual to also tick your (hyperlinked) terms and conditions and privacy notice to keep things legal and decent.

Once you have their contact details you are free to stay in touch and also phone them until they withdraw their consent. Just make sure your privacy notice (or policy) always provides a consent opt-out mechanism, which is as easy for them to withdraw from as it was for them to agree. If you are in Europe, you'll also need to list people's data subject rights and be GDPR compliant.

In SME B2B marketing this kind of campaign will yield sales leads and when run as part of an integrated marketing campaign, will generate even more sales leads, although don't expect vast numbers because your markets are relatively niche.

Key points and actions you need to take from this chapter

1 - Understand the concept of permission marketing
2 - Permission marketing works but needs to be part of an integrated marketing campaign
3 - Don't expect to generate millions of B2B sales leads through permission marketing
4 - Make sure you are compliant with all relevant legislation like GDPR

1 Seth Godin is an American writer and has written around 17 books, addressing various aspects of marketing, advertising, business venturing and leadership

Chapter 21

Branding, why spending a lot on B2B won't give you a return on investment

B2B branding provides the glue that links together each of the integrated marketing components to make clear the identity of the business no matter the marketing activity.

American chef, restaurateur, television personality and author Geoffrey Zakarian says: "Determine who you are and what your brand is, and what you're not. The rest of it is just a lot of noise." Arguably in B2B branding Zakarian may have an important point.

The concept of branding is relatively simple, the brand tells a story about a goal, dream and/or success and hey presto, someone buys the product or service. The storyline, which may also include heritage messages about the founder, is reflected on the product, in its packaging, signage, blogs and PR material. If you have seen Coca-Cola branding with its distinctive red printing, robust packaging and messages like 'Good Times' with a bottle after the Good, you'll note that the overall aim is to leave a positive lasting imprint on the buyer's mind. The Coca-Cola storyboard is all about promoting happiness and the bringing together of friends and families, in effect it is selling a positive dream rather than just a beverage. But is this relevant to the B2B sector?

B2B companies have long debated the importance of having a unique branding policy. Many CEOs believe that it is a waste of money because unlike a consumer product or service, B2B buyers are conventionally more driven by cost, the quality of the service and its availability. This traditional view is receiving challenge from younger and more critical decision makers alongside a move towards global selling, even for small SME companies.

The branding for B2B products is very different to consumer products. Whilst consumers may get excited at the packaging of the latest Apple iPhone, as Apple has made it as artistic and visually appealing as the phone inside, how does this work for Civil Aerospace companies, such as Rolls-Royce?

As an example, Korean airline Air Premia has purchased Rolls-Royce Trent 1000 engines to power 10 Boeing 787 Dreamliner aircraft, however, I can't imagine the engines arriving in an Apple type box with delayed opening, so the engineers working for Boeing can drool over the finer workings of the engines inside!

The branding of B2B differs from B2C as a result of a number of factors. This reflects the longer buying cycle, the fact that the requirements are often predefined by the buyer, the goods or even service are typically far more expensive and there are generally multiple people involved in the buying decision, the stakes are therefore much higher.

Companies like Air Premia and Rolls-Royce tend to adopt a long-term partnership approach because both will have contractual responsibilities to each other during the lifespan of the engines. To address this, B2B companies tend to use branding as a way of strengthening business strategies, rather than the product or service.

So, a business like HubSpot will use its website to highlight its 78,700 customers in over 120 countries and its award-winning support. IBM uses branded social media to talk about its history and products, FedEx showcases its efficacy and most leading B2B companies promote themselves as trustworthy brands. The overall aim is to build their branding around trustworthiness, in order to create brand loyalty.

Rebrands happen for a number of reasons; these can be caused by the sale of the business to another well-established brand, mixed messaging by the current branding or a need to convey a much stronger brand identity. These rebranding exercises can also be management driven following the appointment of new senior employees, who wish to make their own mark on the business.

In terms of a financial return from a complete rebrand, unless your business has an unhelpful trading name, say for our fictious insurance firm 'do little and dally inc' or needs to reflect the branding of a new parent company, my advice is to go for incremental changes, as this allows for opportunities to leverage anything good from the current branding.

Starting a B2B rebrand can be a big exercise and it can add little, if anything, in the short term to the bottom line of the business, so it is often a straight cost. Therefore, your business needs to be clear at the onset about what it wants to achieve from the rebrand and the amount of money it has to invest.

A logical starting point is to determine what marketing messages need conveying and what type of storyline should be attached. The marketing messages might be based around the values of the business such as ethics, the business founder's self-belief and/or the innovative nature of the company. Developing these will need an element of brainstorming and research. As Lisa Gansky[1] so ably put it: "A brand is a voice and a product is a souvenir."

Undertake a survey or consultation process with your existing customers and ask them to tell you what they see as distinctive about your company, this is important because the branding should reflect the experience your customers would like from the business. Once these core facts have been distilled out, it is then possible to instruct a specialist branding or marketing agency to develop some storyboards to convey the key messages in slogans, values and color for bench testing.

This will allow the messages to be bounced off existing customers, employees and other stakeholders. If you are exporting you will also need to ensure, through your agents and/or international sales team, that the branding does not have any negative connotations. For example, when Chevrolet and Lada targeted a Nova car model at the Spanish market, they forgot to check this out, had they done so they would have discovered that 'no va' translates into 'doesn't work!'

In B2B branding there are a few key points to be noted. The first is that any branding should not be restricted to just products; it needs to be used on everything from business cards, to literature, signage, the website, social media and exhibition stands. Secondly the branding must be practical and should have a feel of durability to reflect the longevity of your products and service.

Depending on the nature of your B2B business, items like logos and slogans must, if applicable, be easily transferable onto engineering machinery, and as anyone who has undertaken this kind of branding will know, attaching stickers to oily equipment does not work and alternatives such as riveted plate or even etching will need to be considered.

Any new branding should be the start of the marketing story not the end, promote the background to the new branding through social media, a press release, website and of course to customers through word of mouth.

Depending on the size of your business you may also want to share this with other stakeholders like investors and last but not least, the most important people in your business, the employees!

Key points and actions you need to take from this chapter

1 - Understand the concept of B2B branding, don't confuse it with B2C branding
2 - The overall aim is to build the branding around trustworthiness, in order to create brand loyalty
3 - Why people rebrand and why it will cost money without

contributing much to the bottom line

4 - Work out what the marketing messages might be, based around the values of the business such as ethics, the business founder's self-belief and/or the innovative nature of the company

5 - Have a consultation process with your existing customers to get them to help with the new branding

6 - After finalizing the branding make sure it will work on literature, products and the website

7 - Tell all stakeholders the reason for rebranding and the story behind it.

1 Lisa Gansky is a US author and business entrepreneur. Lisa was co-founder and CEO of Global Network Navigator and co-founder, CEO and chairman of Ofo

Chapter 22

Telemarketing: doing it cost effectively even if you don't want to make the calls

Telesales is one of the key pillars of the integrated marketing circle, without telemarketing there would be no effective campaign. Phone calling is a key link and allows B2B to directly engage with potential customers. Whilst marketing purists may argue it is a sales function, without telesales there would be no integrated marketing.

Robert Louis Stevenson once said: "Everyone lives by selling something." Although sales presentation skills trainer Patricia Fripp[1] puts it a little more precisely for the purposes of this chapter: "It is not your customer's job to remember you. It is your obligation and responsibility to make sure they don't have the chance to forget you."

In marketing utopia, all marketing would be perfect because those wanting to sell certain goods and services would speak to those wanting to buy the same goods and services. Supply and demand would be effortlessly matched and nobody would need to cold call. Unfortunately, no such state exists and therefore the onus is on you, the seller, to identify potential buyers.

Telesales, although technically a sales function rather than a marketing activity, is a critical part of the B2B marketing campaign, because unlike consumer campaigns there is usually/ always a limited number of prospects. In fact telesales is so important, especially when you are dealing with small quantities of data, that if you don't want to make the calls yourself, you hire a temp (temporary staff member) from one of the reputable recruitment agencies, such as, if you are based in the UK, Travail Employment Group. Travail has branches in 26 towns and cities and generally has someone on the books, with some sales experience, who will come for a day or few days, to follow up on your sales leads at an hourly rate. As an added bonus if you really like the temp, the agency will often do a deal allowing you to recruit them, allowing you to test before you buy.

However, if you do hire someone temporarily or permanently to help you, it is really important that you give them a detailed brief and then work closely with them whilst they make your business phone calls. Whatever you decide, you must read this chapter otherwise you may not grasp what needs to be done.

It might be useful at this stage in the process to recap the progress to date before talking in detail about telemarketing which involves, metaphorically speaking, some heavy lifting.

In the earlier chapters we have identified potential customers via purchased prospecting data. We have discussed the importance of identifying the relevant purchasing decision maker at each company, put together an email or postal letter and sent it to each prospect. After the passage of two posting days, or a few hours from sending the email, we are now in the optimum position for following up.

As part of the wider marketing effort we have also drafted either a press release or case study and sent it to the trade and regional media for, hopefully, publishing.

This chapter is now about the heavy lifting because the success or failure of the campaign will rest on your effectiveness in diligently following up each prospect by phone. Unsuccessful contact should be followed by repeat phone calls to a maximum of five.

Providing you have followed the earlier guidance regarding the email or letter, the prospects that need following up should be relevant to your product or service and each company should have been alerted to the fact that you will be following them up thanks to your e-marketing letter or posted marketing mailer.

The list of companies for following up should be held in a

contact management database or a spreadsheet that has a spare column so that you can add follow-up notes.

The first point of contact is likely to be a receptionist or some other type of gatekeeper, whose primary purpose is to interrogate callers to ensure only the right calls get through to those who matter, i.e., those already known to the contact, such as existing suppliers and to block the speculative callers like you. I don't blame companies for doing this because time is money, but if you want to make every call count an element of strategy is required.

When the receptionist asks you if the contact is expecting your call say yes you are already in correspondence and that he or she is expecting your call.

This is perfectly true because you agreed to contact them in your e-marketing letter or postal letter. Some receptionists will put the call through based on that premise whilst others will ask more searching questions. Always be courteous, never lose your temper, ensure you note the name of the receptionist and no matter what they say always end the call on a positive note by politely thanking them for their helpfulness.

If you get asked what the call is regarding, say it's a sensitive matter but that you have emailed over the details already. If the receptionist still refuses to play ball, you'll need to log the call on your database or spreadsheet and come back to the call later in the day. The second call should be attempted at 12.30pm (lunchtime), as a guide more junior staff tend to still get a lunchbreak between 12pm and 1 pm. This, of course, presupposes that the receptionist is a junior employee and qualifies for a lunch break, because if he or she is part time they may only be covering say 9am until 3pm allowing them to exit promptly for childcare duties. Either way this could be to your advantage.

If this second attempt fails, log the response on your database or spreadsheet and call after 3pm on the following day. If you still get the same receptionist answering the call, ask for the accounts department and just give your firm's name. Most companies are only too grateful that someone would like to talk to their accounts department and most receptionists will never grill their callers. On connection with accounts ask them for the department and the name of the person you would like to speak with and ask if they can put you straight through.

In some case the receptionist won't be able to connect you with your target contact because they might not be around. In the B2B sector it is not uncommon for senior members of staff to spend a lot of time on the factory floor or in something like the company's operations room, especially if your target company is also looking to launch its own new product or service.

In subsequent follow up communication, a little bit of common sense applies. Start work through the list of contacts at about 9.15am if possible and continue until your lunchbreak. More senior decision makers will either work through lunch or take a break at around 1pm which is when you should have a break. Telephone work is exhaustive so ensure you take regular breaks and keep yourself hydrated with coffee, tea or water.

A significant proportion of the people you are calling won't be available or will refuse to take the call, this is very normal, so whilst my advice is to call 100 companies per day, it is unlikely that you will have more than 25 meaningful calls per day. This will require four days to be devoted to the work although the latter two days will most likely be part days.

From personal experience the most productive days to start a campaign are Tuesday or Wednesday.

If your calls don't reach the target audience, please try and find out from the receptionist when your contact will be back at their office desk. Again, if the receptionist is not too forthcoming try different times. If the target contact's firm opens at 8.30am, try calling at 8.40am and if this still doesn't succeed, try calling at different time intervals during the course of the working day.

This whole procedure may sound very frustrating and it is, but please do remember the harder the person is to reach the more senior and possibly receptive they will be.

If you have made at least five attempts at different times of the day and have followed the process outlined, then you have no alternative but to move on to one of the other target companies.

One of the biggest reasons these campaigns fail is that the people following up run out of persistence and just give up. However, within your target list there will be at least one or two people who will be interested in your product or service, the challenge is reaching them.

A short while ago I decided to look at Project Management software, I prepared a shortlist of potential suppliers using the internet and software reviews as a guide. Coincidently in the midst of contacting two potential suppliers, I received a telephone call from another software supplier. They claimed to have spoken with me two years ago and had me on a list of prospects, although in all honesty I couldn't remember, because like many business people I have a job remembering last week, let alone two years ago.

After a very good conversation, I invited the company to do a presentation; I liked the product and due to a great offer, signed a contract the very same afternoon. Timing is everything with all marketing projects and coincidently my new supplier had phoned precisely at the very hour I was looking for a new supplier.

Therefore, for all the knocks, moans and rejections, someone, somewhere will require your product and your task is making the follow up calls to find them.

Let us now suppose that you have reached your contact, the subsequent conversation must be handled in a professional and confident way. Please don't start the conversation, which is becoming more frequent and annoying, by asking the contact "how are you today?"

Explain who you are and tell the contact that you sent them an email or letter around a day ago. Don't be surprised if your contact doesn't remember the letter. If they don't recall the document or email still press on and in a sentence (no more than two), describe the product or service you are promoting.

Most people in B2B are very busy but will listen to your proposition; a very small minority will terminate the call by putting down the telephone. In my experience on 200 calls, two or three will be rude and one may just abruptly terminate. However, here's the thing, if you are following the prescriptive methods outlined in this book, based on 100 calls, two or three people will definitely be interested (unless your targeting is defective) and will most likely go on to have a demonstration and/or buy your goods or services.

Making any phone call can be stressful so pace the work out, make a supreme effort to make at least 100 calls a day and if you are feeling nervous don't be afraid to stand up when you make a call. The effect of standing up allows your lungs to fully inflate and this allows a much less nervous performance.

It is likely that the contact person you are talking with will raise objections, take this as encouragement because at least they are conversing with you. Don't think of customer objections as rejections. Instead, think of them as engagement opportunities. Try and be as transparent as possible. The more the sales prospects trust and feel comfortable with you or your telemarketing person, the more likely they are to express any objections, which will then give you the opportunity to overcome them.

Before engaging on the telephone follow-up, it is worth rehearsing in your head or with a colleague the type of objections that might get raised and the answers that would need to be given to overcome them.

Remember, this chapter is not about turning you into a super sales person but it is about helping you get the best productivity from the time devoted to the telephone follow-up.

Try and see telephone calling as a very necessary part of the job, even if you don't want to do it just pace yourself and try. The most ardent advocate of your product or service is likely to be you, not a junior staff member or outside telemarketing agency.

Depending on your business proposition, it may be as simple as gaining the trust of the contact and sending a quote that will need following up, or the start of a more sophisticated marketing process that involves some kind of meeting.

Each phone call should have a purpose and no matter how hard the prospect tries you should re-anchor them back to what you wish to achieve, whether this is getting information to complete a quote, arranging an onsite meeting, visit to your premises, webinar or a virtual meeting using something like Zoom or GoToMeeting.

Whatever you promise the sales prospect always try and complete it sooner, so if you commit to sending a quote on the Friday, send it on the Thursday. If you promise to call back at 2pm make sure you call back at precisely 2pm. These small acts are confidence builders with your sales prospect and it allows you to demonstrate that you are dependable, because nobody wants to deal with a company that is unreliable, although few will ever be so blunt as to tell you that.

The challenge is not to talk yourself out of doing the sales calls, or more aptly doing the heavy lifting. As Sir Edmund Hillary said: "It is not the mountain we conquer but ourselves."

Key points and actions you need to take from this chapter

1 - If you personally don't want to do the follow-up, hire a temporary member of staff who does

2 - There is often a finite number of prospects, don't waste

them by not doing the phone work this book advocates

3 - Respect the people you are calling, don't be glib on the phone, make sure you have sent the mailer and then make it clear you are following up on that mailer, if they haven't got it send again and then quickly re-follow up

4 - 100 calls that result in a conversation will normally generate between 3 and 12 sales leads

5 - Everyone who has been correctly identified is a potential sales prospect so make sure you stay in touch with them after the call, by adding their details to your mailing lists

1 Patricia Fripp, American management consultant, trainer and author of various publications including *Get What You Want!*

Chapter 23

Trade Shows and how to avoid pouring money down the drain

For most B2B there is at least one annual event, and in some industries multiple opportunities, to exhibit. Whilst exhibiting or even attending a show as a visitor is not a critical part of integrated marketing or one of the key pillars, it is a marketing component and it would therefore be rather remiss of me, when writing a book of this nature not to include a brief section on exhibitions.

According to Bruce Carlisle, CEO of Conference Hound, a conference discovery platform, there are based on his best guess up to one million individual events worldwide, every year, ranging from the very large to relatively small exhibitions.

It would also be fair to say that trade exhibitions provide a wide range of marketing opportunities. Exhibitors allow companies not only to find potential new customers but to have business meetings, cultivate a marketing image, discover business partners, for example, distributors and learn more about a particular market. These same rules apply to visitors, who can survey the market, find suppliers, compare prices and sales terms, test out new products and explore opportunities for doing business.

Trade shows started as a result of the industrial revolution, most are annual events generally held at the same time each year unless disrupted by war and public health issues like Covid-19.

For many B2B businesses involved in supplying machinery, although less so for service providers, trade shows are a popular way to showcase new equipment to a large audience based at one location. Whilst it would be nearly impossible to take a large machine on tour round the country or continent, the problem is solved by potential customers coming to you, through their attendance at the exhibition.

A lot of the show management/burden is handled by the organizers and whilst exhibiting is always very disruptive to companies, it can generally be managed over a week or ten days and then the company can start to return back to normal.

The performance of the exhibition is easy to calculate based on the number of sales leads generated and how many are converted into sales leads, which makes it popular with senior decision makers.

Many exhibition venues also provide important value-added services like electricity, attendee badge scanners, pre-designed booths, opportunities for speaking, mailing lists, that all important show guide and often a show mailer.

In recent years there has been a re-emergence of tabletop shows, these provide the exhibitor with the equivalent space of a table on which to promote their wares. These shows by their very nature are more restrictive, but are also cheaper. Apart from price the main advantage of these table top shows is that only limited equipment can be exhibited so the shows are generally far less demanding. However, the payback is often that the attendance of a more generic audience may not be as relevant to your company's marketing messages.

There are a number of websites that list exhibitions and if you are unsure complete a Google search or take a look at these websites:

UK: https://www.expocart.com/exhibition/calendar
   or https://www.tradefairdates.com
US: https://10times.com/top100/usa
Australia: https://10times.com/australia/tradeshows
Canada: https://10times.com/top100/canada

In determining whether or not to exhibit at a particular show, if possible, try and attend the show as a visitor prior to making a commitment. This allows you to get a feel as to whether the right kind of attendees for your goods or services are at the show and whether your competitors or companies offering complementary services are also exhibiting. Secondly, consult the show's website to see whether exhibitors offering the same product or services are multiple exhibitors at the show, or have attended as a one-off. This is important because if other competing companies attend each exhibition, it implies a return on investment.

It should be noted that some shows can deliberately create a sub culture that some individuals find gratifying, such as evening drinks parties, an exhibitors' dinner, VIP tickets for lunches or other perks during the exhibition. It is important that your judgement is not clouded by the recognition factor these can provide, ultimately you must judge the show on the number of sales leads it provides and your ability to convert these leads into orders.

Let's suppose you have done your research and decided to exhibit at a particular show. The first big question is when you should book the stand (or booth in the US) and the second is what size stand should be booked?

Many show organizers give an early bird discount, which allows you to book a stand in a decent location whilst also getting a good deal. This is often the best route, providing you can get a reasonable discount, but try to negotiate the payment terms phased over a number of months.

Determining the best location is always tricky, popular locations are near show cafes, speaking events, leisure areas and anywhere else that has a reasonably high footfall.

The third point to make is that exhibition stands are expensive, so it is always wise to start modest and build towards a bigger stand the following year. Of course, the show organizers will be keen to sell you the biggest stand possible, but I would advise you to hold your ground, certainly until you are confident of the returns you receive.

Push the organizers for value added things such as free editorial coverage in any mailer piece that they are circulating, free support from the PR agency promoting the show and of course some free speaking opportunities.

All exhibitions are time demanding and expensive so it is important that you squeeze as much as possible out of the show. This should include doing a press release at least three months before the show for the trade media (see chapter 13), highlighting your company's attendance on social media, your website and any other relevant outlets. It is also important that you write a decent entry for the show catalogue and get this to the organizers well before the copy deadline. Finally, establish if there is a pressroom where you can upload your show press release, pictures and anything else that attendees might find interesting.

Encourage the show organizers to elicit from you company positive comments for their media outlets because these are all free, positive, publicity opportunities.

During the exhibition consider having an on-stand event for journalists to attend at a particular time, so you can tell them more about your business and showcase a particular product or service. This on-stand event should last no more than 15 minutes, your presentation needs to be concise and informative with the opportunity for at least five minutes of questions at the end. Don't forget that the journalists can, of course, be incentivized to attend your firm's on-stand presentation through offering a free bottle of wine for collection at the stand, following the presentation, for them to take home!

Having covered the off-stand marketing, effort is also needed to decide on the theme of your stand and the equipment or service you plan to exhibit. The theme will be largely dictated by the size of your stand. For booth type formats, typically 5 x 3 meters, the theme will be somewhat limited as the organizers will typically provide a white emulsioned semi-enclosed stand with a standard name board and some kind of carpeting. Therefore, your choice of theme will need to be conveyed through roller banners, popup backdrops and product branding.

The biggest challenge with all exhibitions is how to engage with a fluid audience, I have attended shows and possibly you have too, where exhibitors looking tired and bored, are hunched over a laptop computer in the vain hope that any visitors will go away!

Anyone providing on stand support must be motivated and willing to participate in talking to attendees. People passing the stand should be engaged in conversation and all show visitors encouraged to enter a prize draw for a bottle of champagne, to be drawn on the last day of the show. Where available visitor badge scanning should be deployed as it will save time in the long run, providing you have an accurate record concerning the product or service of interest.

During the Covid-19 lockdown, one of the first casualities was trade exhibitions due to the risks posed by the pandemic. This has triggered a massive rise in virtual business meetings using technologies like Teams, GoToMeeting and Zoom, and also an increase in demand for virtual exhibitions. Although still in its infancy virtual exhibitions are here for the short term and if they can attract sufficient audiences, which is still to be determined, also for the long run. It is also likely that the technology will be used to bolster audience numbers at future physical shows.

The cost benefits of virtual shows are significant but the issue B2B companies struggle with is getting prospective customers to engage. So far, the most successful examples are those with recognized interactive speakers who will speak at a particular time which has been well promoted before the appointed hour. The aim is to get your target audience involved in listening to an expert speaker in the hope they will look at some of the equipment or services that you are virtually showcasing at the exhibition.

Post-show all sales leads should be quickly logged into a database and followed up by telephone. Don't be surprised to have to make multiple calls before reaching the people who visited your stand. This is fairly typical but also good news, as I doubt your competitors will make the same level of effort!

If it has been a good exhibition consider buying, post-show, the mailing list of the attendees, however only purchase what you require as outlined in chapters three and four.

Measuring success is all about your return on investment so please ignore the ubiquitous statistics provided by the show organizers, the real acid test is the number of the leads generated for your company and more importantly, how many of these you convert into sales.

Key points and actions you need to take from this chapter

1 - Trade shows are part of the integrated marketing mix but solid homework must be done in advance before booking a particular show

2 - Only book early if you can get some kind of deal and a choice of stand location

3 - Look for valued added incentives from the organizers, such as free publicity or inclusion in mailer pieces

4 - Use PR, the website and social media to highlight your attendance

5 - Consider having a mini on-stand press event to cement your company's relationship with the trade media

6 - Post show, contact all enquiries quickly, if necessary, phone them multiple times

7 - Make sure you set in place some means of measuring success before attending the show otherwise it may all get

lost in the moment

8 - Consider buying the show's attendees list depending on the quality of your initial leads

Chapter 24

Research, doing your homework, where to find marketing information

Time invested in research will help to find demand for your product and/or services before they are launched, it can help your business understand its existing or potential customers, what drives them and stimulates their loyalty – and it can also save significant money on integrated marketing in the longer term.

German and later American aerospace engineer and space architect, Werner von Braun, is credited with saying: "Research is what I'm doing when I don't know what I'm doing." This feels very apt at this point in the discussion.

Many SMEs don't always appreciate that market research does not need to cost a fortune and that by investing time a smaller business can competitively compete against much bigger businesses.

Businesses undertake market research for a variety of reasons, for the purpose of this book we are interested in market research to help your business expand or for start-ups to have a good chance of succeeding. It is worth reflecting that according to Fundera[1] a US based lead generation company, 20% of US small businesses fail in their first year, 30% of small business fail in their second year, and 50% of small businesses fail after five years in business. Finally, 70% of small business owners fail in their 10th year in business. In the UK the figures are similar, 20 per cent will close their doors within just 12 months and 60% of new businesses go under within three years, according to the Daily Telegraph.[2] The reasons vary but the fundamental issue is predominantly always around providing goods or services that customers want and which your business can provide at a profit.

This trading quandary applies to all companies, and some of the world's most successful businesses have all had very shaky starts. It is worth remembering that Amazon was a wobbly business for many years. In 2002, Amazon had long-term debt of $2.2 billion and just $738 million cash. The firm's cash drained as sales stagnated. Armed with little more than a marketing plan and a strong vision by its founder, Jeff Bezos, the company held off bankruptcy and cut its workforce by 14%. By 2003, Amazon had made its first full-year profit of $35 million. Today Amazon is recognized as one of the most successful companies and its founder one of the richest in the world. However, the world didn't bestow this on the business and its founder, they achieved it through ongoing market research, all backed by Bezos' business vision. Sure, it hasn't all been plain sailing for Amazon, the firm has had its share of product flops, the most notable being the Fire smartphone, but it has learnt from the experience and started to focus more on what people wanted. It later used research from watching what other retailers sold on its Amazon Marketplace, to start selling the most successful products itself. Although a simple research strategy, it was able to learn using its own platform, from some of the most successful retailers and then compete with them by offering the same products.

For those with an established business the starting point for market research is to consult your existing customer base and then take a look at the competition. Most SMEs don't spend much, if any, time consulting their existing customers, why would they? The majority of effort is put into fulfilling contractual obligations and their senior management's time keeping the customer happy when things go wrong. Some firms will have a marketing planning day and may even have an annual brainstorming session. Nonetheless, often the marketing doesn't change much and the same marketing plans are simply given a fresh coat of paint.

This results in these firms attending the same exhibitions and often getting the same mediocre trading results year after year! However, if you could drill down and consult your customers and potential customers about the different aspects of your business, you could start to develop a strategic marketing plan based on fact rather than wishful thinking.

You can seek the opinion of your customers on a wide variety of topics, such as the appeal of your current website, what social media they use, which trade publications they read or what they think of your existing communications such as newsletters and emails. As in all these situations, the more relevant and precise the information gained the better the chances of developing a strategic marketing plan that works. Determining the correct questions to ask will lead the direction of your marketing plan.

In addition, we also need to learn more about the existing customers in terms of their own business demographics. This is because whether you are an existing business or just starting up, you need to try and develop a customer profile. This is harder for start-up businesses, but it is even more vital that your company knows who its target audience is. What industry sectors are your customers or potential customers located within, what size turnover, employee numbers, geographical location and finally which decision maker do you need to reach? Remember this could be a multitude of job titles - see chapters three and four for more guidance.

The aim is to create a customer profile from the information you already know about them and from further follow-up research.

It is also worth remembering that just like you your customers and potential customers are continuing to evolve with changing needs and expectations, so their position this month could be very different in six months time, so it is important to regularly undertake research, rather than seeing it as a onetime event.

Mechanisms for the research

One of the easiest ways of understanding the views of your customers, is to undertake a survey using SurveyMonkey, or a comparable digital solution. This is an online platform which is available for free at the entry level format and allows the user to create and send a survey with up to 10 questions or elements. A variety of question types, descriptive text and images can be included. The benefit of SurveyMonkey is that it depersonalizes the answers and provides collective responses to the different questions, this avoids the issues becoming personal, unless you wish to drill down. It is worth remembering, the greater the number of questions, the lower the number of respondents, so it is better to ask ten questions rather than 50. Spend some time refining and testing the questions to make sure responses will be relevant. Remember you can always do a follow-up survey at a later date.

The next step is to look at your competitors and try and benchmark your own company against the averages of those competitors. This should allow you to measure the performance of your own business, over time, against typical firms in your industry. Some of these firms will be sluggish and others will be performing well. Using this data, reading trade journals and looking at competitors' websites you may get some customer names in terms of who they supply. Clearly, it stands to reason that you want to have customers in the sectors where your competitors are doing well, rather than toiling.

Information concerning competitors can be found from a number of sources, in the UK, Companies House, in the US and Canada the Federal Authorities or in Australia the ASIC and New Zealand the Securities & Investment Commission, as highlighted earlier in this book.

There are also a small number of very capable credit rating agencies who have simplified extracting this data like Creditsafe in the UK or internationally Dun & Bradstreet, who can provide financial data relating to performance. Remember the volume of direct competitors will hopefully be no more than a handful. The follow-up step is to look at the overall market which your customers are trading within and your firm's competitors are targeting.

Let's suppose you want to know more information about the meat pie sector, especially producers of pork pies because you want to supply them with a pastry machine. As a starting point see if there are any relevant Trade Associations. In the UK there is the Melton Mowbray Pork Pie Association and the Guild of Fine Food, both represent a cross-section of artisan producers. In Australia there is the Baking Association and, in the US, the American Pie Council (APC). Each of these organizations can provide information about events which will be attended by members, some sites even provide member details. Other useful information can often be found on their websites and on social media such as Facebook. Don't forget to follow these members on Twitter and to engage with them on Facebook and LinkedIn, when your strategy has been finalized.

A follow-up action is to try and quantify the number of producers, by searching Companies House in the UK, the Federal Authorities in the US and Canada or the ASIC in Australia and the Securities & Investment Commission in New Zealand. The best way to do this is to identify the SIC code of existing customers or in the US the NAICS code. In the UK the 2007 SIC Code 10130 comprises those involved in the production of meat and poultry meat products, which includes meat pies. Alternatively, you can use what is generically titled industry directory (see chapter three for more details).

I would recommend having a look at some of the database suppliers' websites to get a (free) overview for the potential number of customers you could target. In the UK Selectabase or in the US, Canada, Australia and New Zealand Kompass or Harvest Business Lists - all have some basic online data information or list builder that you can access for free. See appendices for their contact details.

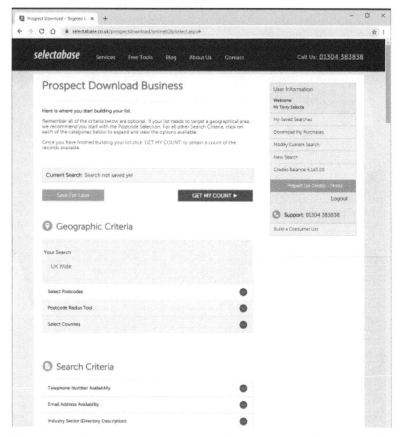

Now you know your target audience, depending on the marketing budget, research companies like OnePoll can be commissioned to undertake a survey on behalf of your business. This can provide valuable information such as top-level data indicating whether a sector is in expansion or decline and more detailed statistics about future expansion plans.

When the customer research has been completed you should have an understanding of the likely decision-making process and how customers go about finding information on products and services. Consider creating a customer persona to use.

Once all the research and customer profiling has been completed it is important to use the data to create a strategic marketing plan which will enable the business objectives and goals to be set. These can then be fine-tuned during the course of a twelve-month period. Ideally your plan should be segmented into monthly and quarterly deliverables.

Key points and actions you need to take from this chapter

1 - Understand the value of good research, you can do the legwork so it doesn't need to cost a fortune
2 - With accurate data you can start to build a business around facts rather than suppositions
3 - Talk to your existing or potential customers, better to ask them ten well thought out questions than 50 random questions. Spend some time refining and testing them to make sure responses will be relevant.
4 - Look at your competitors, how are they performing? What are they doing well?
5 - Investigate whether your potential customers are a member of a relevant trade body or association, as these organizations can be a rich source of potential sales leads and other useful information
6 - Look at the free data on the websites of database suppliers to test how big your potential customer market might be
7 - Consider using a research company like OnePoll to help develop some breadth and sector segmentation
8 - Use all the data collected to develop a marketing plan segmented into monthly and quarterly campaigns

1 https://www.fundera.com/blog/what-percentage-of-small-businesses-fail
2 https://www.telegraph.co.uk/politics/2019/01/24/start-ups-across-uk-going-bust-need-careful-management-economy/

Chapter 25

ROI: what is your return on investment? How to monitor the campaign

To make marketing campaigns more viable it is vital that you adopt integrated marketing as explained in this book, because if each of the marketing activities undertaken can be used to spin one, two or even three more plates, the return on the marketing investment (ROI) will be so much higher.

"Ideas are great. Execution rocks. Knowing the ROI amplifies the contributions of everyone involved and keeps stakeholders happy," so says Leena Patel, author, innovation consultant and CEO of Sandbox2Boardroom.com.

Ok, so this chapter has the potential to be the dullest of all but I will try to keep it cheery, because if there was a marketing topic that is the most misunderstood, ignored and sometimes abused it has to be ROI. But please don't blame me, blame the accountants who have developed some pretty dull terminology.

In its crudest format, ROI tries to directly measure the amount of return on a specific marketing investment, relative to the actual cost of the marketing. This is normally correlated around sales growth minus the cost of the marketing.

Typically, the ROI is calculated using two primary systems of measurement: the cost of delivering the marketing program and the outcomes generated as a result. (This is typically measured in profit, although many companies will settle for turnover or revenue.)

The standard ROI formula comprises: (Attributable sales increase - marketing cost) divided by the marketing cost = ROI as a percentage.

So, if sales have increased by $500,000 and the cost of marketing was $50,000:

(500,000 – 50,000)

50000   = 9% ROI

The ROI would be 9%

This formula doesn't of course, take into account the profit generated, which after taking into account overheads and other margins will be much lower than $450,000. Therefore, as an absolute minimum return, your business needs to cover the cost of making the product or providing the service and making a profit. Most businesses should be looking for a 5:1 ratio for an acceptable return, although remember, profits may be much higher if the customer purchases repeat orders, has a service contract and/or continues spending with your business after the first year.

However, the problem with ROI for marketeers and their cheerleaders - the sales team, is that there are always caveats resulting in the formation of opinions based often on little more than anecdotal information. For example, "Sure the marketing secured a sale but Jim has been talking to that customer for two years." "We are having a great year, it must be down to the $50,000 we invested in advertising, what were the names of the publications we went with again?"

In both the above examples, people are making subjective statements on sales successes without being able to quantify the impact of the marketing. Over my career I have heard these statements many times over.

As a B2B company, whether you are the managing director or marketing assistant you need to be able to answer one very simple question, what result is the business achieving from its marketing?

Despite the formula presented earlier in this chapter, there can never be a precise formula, because an accurate answer needs to be based around a number of variables, beyond just increased sales.

The first involves knowing what to measure and when. It should also be noted that there is almost always a time lag between the money being invested into marketing and when it provides a result. For example, sales leads for capital equipment from an exhibition can take up to twelve months and even longer if it involves capital expenditure. Therefore, quantifying four weeks after an exhibition to determine if it was a success is too early, and equally deciding to rebook the show four weeks after attending would also be premature.

The reality is that the money you invest today will have an uncertain impact at an uncertain point in the future. Let's look at some of the factors:

Target companies can have multiple influencers, these are people who have in-depth knowledge, interest or insight into a specific subject. In larger companies, whilst these people may not be directly purchasing the product or service, they could be a board member, key employee such as a production manager or even a consultant, whatever their role, it is likely that they will hold some kind of sway. Understanding and measuring which marketing program had the most influence is also a big challenge.

Marketeers often talk about multiple touches, the raison d'être behind this theory is that at least seven marketing touches are needed to turn a cold sales lead into an actual sale. Each touch represents a marketing activity involving the target customer, however, allocating the income generated from the sale to each of the touches is almost impossible!

There are almost always extraneous variables, which are often outside the control of the marketing program. As an example, during the first two months of the Covid-19 crisis, the sale of bread and pastries in the UK(1) and US(2) increased by a massive amount over sales earlier in the year. How many bakery machinery suppliers sold additional equipment as production machinery started failing as a result of increased usage?

At the same time, how many packaging machinery companies sold more equipment when a social media scare about toilet rolls caused supermarket shelves to be stripped almost overnight of supplies, forcing the suppliers' toilet rolls to increase production all of which required packaging?

Other factors such as a change in the public's behavior, the weather, and even the appointment of more sales people, can have a favorable or unfavorable impact on sales and can therefore distort the integrated marketing program's ROI.

To take into account each of these different factors a multiple measuring of ROI is needed that results in a grand total at the end.

This means looking at results from the different core marketing components. As already highlighted as a potential issue, new customers will have multiple touches as part of your integrated marketing campaign. Many of these marketing components have their own built-in ROI, although taken in isolation each will most likely provide spurious results. For example, YouTube will tell you that only 50 people watched a video about your new machine, but if the traffic was driven to YouTube from a press release, twitter link or even a telesales phone call and just one person purchases a machine as a result, that is most likely a great outcome.

To correlate everything together you will need some kind of matrix and I have developed a simple chart on the next page, for you to modify as necessary, to get to grips with performance monitoring. However, a word of caution, removing some of the least effective components may impact on the number of touches, this is because there will be a push pull relationship between them, so for example Twitter or a press release could create increased website traffic, therefore changes should be made sequentially, as your business experiments to find the most cost-effective results.

Social Media	Measurements	Enquiries	Sales	Cost
Twitter	Followers, retweets, direct comments and mail	Level of customer engagement or website traffic created	Volume of direct sales enquiries and sales created	Labor and any other costs
Facebook	Likes, comments	Level of customer engagement or website traffic created	Volume of direct sales enquiries and sales created	Labor and any other costs
LinkedIn	Likes, InMail, others	Level of customer engagement or website traffic created	Volume of direct sales enquiries and sales created	Labor and any other costs
YouTube	Views, comments	Level of customer engagement or website traffic created	Volume of direct sales enquiries and sales created	Labor and any other costs such as making the video
Digital Comms	Measurements	Enquiries	Sales	Cost
Digital Mailers	Read receipts, clicking links, website activity	Level of customer engagement or website traffic created	Volume of direct sales enquiries and sales created	Labor and any other costs such as design costs, payment for the platform and distribution costs
Newsletter	Read receipts, clicking links, website activity, customer comments	Level of customer engagement or website traffic created	Volume of direct sales enquiries and sales created	Labor and any other costs such as writing, design, payment for the platform and distribution costs
Media Activities	Measurements	Enquiries	Sales	Cost
Press releases	Cuttings, volume of publications the article has appeared within, customer comments	Level of customer engagement or website traffic created	Volume of direct sales enquiries and sales created	Labor and any other costs such as writing and color separation costs
Case studies	Cuttings, volume of publications the article has appeared within	Level of customer engagement or website traffic created	Volume of direct sales enquiries and sales created	Labor and any other costs such as writing and color separation costs
Features	Size of coverage, customer comments	Level of customer engagement or website traffic created	Volume of direct sales enquiries and sales created	Labor and any other costs such as writing and color separation costs

Online				
Website	Number of visitors and visitor dwell time	Level of customer engagement	Volume of direct sales enquiries and sales created	Hosting fees, time updating the content and any cost associated with adding pages
SEO work	Increased website visitors	Level of customer engagement or extra website traffic created	Volume of direct sales enquiries and sales created	Cost of using a SEO specialist
Advertising	Measurements	Enquiries	Sales	Cost
Facebook	Number of clicks	Level of customer engagement or extra website traffic created	Volume of direct sales enquiries and sales created	Labor to set the system up and advert costs
LinkedIn	Number of clicks	Level of customer engagement or extra website traffic created	Volume of direct sales enquiries and sales created	Labor to set the system up and advert costs
Google Ads	Ratio of people clicking the ads to those visiting the website	Level of customer engagement or extra website traffic created	Volume of direct sales enquiries and sales created	Labor to set the system up and advert costs
On page advertising	Total publication readership, accuracy i.e. ABC audited	Level of customer engagement or extra website traffic created	Volume of direct sales enquiries and sales created	Design of adverts and cost of advertising
Exhibitions	Measurements	Enquiries	Sales	Cost
Show 1 etc	Number of on stand visitors	The number of enquiries generated, quality of sales leads	Number of sales created	Heavy labor costs to set the stand up and manage the event, often involving additional subsistence costs
Telesales	Measurements	Enquiries	Sales	Cost
Campaign 1 etc	Number of calls	The number of enquiries generated	Number of sales created	Cost of employee or contractor, any additional support costs
Monthly Summary for past month	Number of integrated marketing activities undertaken	Total number of enquiries	Total number of sales	Total cost of marketing to generate the leads

Remember as already stated, the chart is just a starting point, so it may need additional components adding and a few creating. Although slightly fiddly, it will need updating each month and will need some modest inputs from the sales team.

In addition to calculating the traditional ROI as expressed at the start of this chapter, other calculations can be made. An alternative way of measuring the marketing is to strip everything back to the individual marketing components, based on a cost per sales lead (CPL) and then to calculate how many leads are required to generate one sale. This is again slightly subjective because it depends how strong the leads are and how effective the sales staff are at converting them. These would include:

Total value of sales less cost of sales = X

Number of sales divided by cost = the amount each sale has cost

Enquiries divided by sales = the sales conversion ratio

Ultimately, as long as you are diligently measuring results each month and then start tweaking the integrated marketing to allocate the resources towards increasing the number of sales, your business is moving in the right direction. It is also worth remembering that the business may be affected by seasonal fluctuations and the number of working days in each month, with December often being the shortest, so once a year has been completed, please do compare month on month for the previous year.

Key points and actions you need to take from this chapter

1 - Understand the ROI formula

2 - Avoid subjective analysis and work with facts based on effective business measures

3 - Understand the cost of marketing to the cost of the sale

4 - Grasp the concept of multiple touches, it is key to successful integrated marketing
5 - Produce a replica of the graph encompassing all individual marketing activities
6 - Also look at the CPL which may give a simpler way of explaining the performance of marketing
7 - Ensure that you measure each month and after a year compare the previous year's month with the current month
8 - Make incremental changes to the integrated marketing campaign

1 https://www.statista.com/statistics/1114072/coronavirus-covid-19-sales-changes-uk/
2 https://www.americanbakers.org/2020/03/bakery-sales-jump/

Chapter 26

Professional budgeting, keeping it simple and effective

Deciding on the size of your marketing budget is always a big challenge, especially if you are a start-up firm or a SME and have never budgeted previously. Running integrated marketing works considerably better with reliable data on marketing expenditure and allows the cost of your integrated marketing to be measured against actual sales results.

"What is the value to a marketer of insight that isn't implemented? Zero," says author and award-winning marketing ROI researcher, Rex Briggs.

A good starting point is to create a budget spreadsheet and to link this over time with the value or actual gross profit of the sales generated. A common challenge for most businesses is what percentage of turnover should be allocated for marketing purposes. Various figures have been suggested and these range from 20% of turnover to as little as 0.5%.

In the B2B sector in the UK a top-level budget of around 5% would be relatively typical. As you will note, this says top level because UK marketers have a history of not including some of the peripheral promotional costs, especially where labor might be split between more than one cost center. This might, for example, involve not accounting for the costs of an administrator who has spent two weeks dispatching a mailshot or updating the content of the website.

In the US, marketing costs are often taken more seriously. The CMO of a US Federal registered research agency collects marketing data to allow predictions concerning future markets, track marketing excellence and improve the value of marketing in firms, by surveys, twice yearly. It reports that:

1 - The average US B2B product budget is 8.1% of turnover.

2 - The average US B2B services budget was 7.5% of turnover.

A lot of UK and Australian SME firms mistakenly exclude the cost of planning the campaign, investing in monitoring and tracking the sales effort alone. Whilst this expenditure is unlikely to be significant for smaller firms, as a matter of strategy it is good practice to include some costs for planning, monitoring and tracking as this will enable you to monitor your overall marketing budget much more accurately, or to be blunt less wastefully.

To summarize, work on a total budget of 8% of sales turnover, whether you are based in the US, Canada, Australia, New Zealand, the UK, Ireland or even South Africa. Do include all related costs and do create a detailed marketing plan, so that you can monitor and measure your sales performance against budget.

A simple budget is set out on the adjacent page. My advice at this stage is not to confuse tracking costs with trying to avoid incurring (good) marketing costs. Good marketing costs are those that enable your business to generate new business and penetrate new markets. In a nutshell, it is not the amount you spend, but where and how you spend it and the return from that investment that really matters.

Secondly, don't be tempted to pay a lot of money for a readymade marketing spreadsheet, whilst the information may look slightly more impressive in presentation, it will not make a jot of difference to your marketing campaign and the information that needs to be included can be as easily presented on a standard Excel spreadsheet.

Thirdly and just to reiterate, the principle which is at the core of integrated marketing is that every marketing activity should deliver on at least two components and preferably three marketing items.

For budgetary purposes an assumption has been made that the company is an SME, although clearly with the right tweaking and a few extra columns the spreadsheet could be repopulated for a plc or multinational. The outsourced figures provide a guide, based on what a typical marketing agency might charge in the UK.

Activity	Volume	Budget Year 1 completed in-house	Budget Year 1 outsourced	ROI reflected in the increased sales revenue and profit
Market Research - External agency	1	N/A	$1,500 +	To be added by you
PR - Case studies, press release and features	12	Internal time to complete	$12,000 (includes PR database and distribution costs)	To be added by you
Marketing Databases – Purchasing, verifying, cleansing	Ongoing in batches of 100	$50 per 100 records Internal time to complete	$50 per 100 records External temp labor $15 per hour	To be added by you
Digital Mailer letters - Design of templates Circulation costs	3	Internal time to complete	$100 x 3 $300 $0.025 each	To be added by you
Literature - creation of three A4 single-sided leaflets	3	N/A	$150 x 3 $450	To be added by you

Social Media - Hootsuite		Business Hootsuite $300 per YR	Business Hootsuite $300 per YR	To be added by you
Social media postings: Facebook Twitter LinkedIn YouTube	X 1 per wk day X 1 per wk day X 1 per wk day X 1 per month	Internal time to complete	$10,000 per YR	
Promoted Facebook LinkedIn retargeting campaign	Monthly Monthly	$2,000 per YR $2,000 per YR Plus internal time to complete	$2,000 per YR $2,000 per YR $2,500 per YR	To be added by you
Traditional on page advertising Advert designs	1 advert per month x $1,000 4 per year x A4	$12,000 per YR N/A	$12,000 per YR Agency fee 10% paid by publisher $2,000	To be added by you
Advertising - Google Ads	$300 per month	Monitoring and making changes, your time to complete	Agency fee including monitoring and making changes $2,000 Per YR	To be added by you
Website - Further development work SEO	Ongoing Ongoing	Your time to complete	Ballpark fee $8,000 Per YR	To be added by you
E-newsletters - Creation of templates and management of mailers	4 based on one per quarter	Your time to complete	Design, writing and circulating $1,500 per issue	To be added by you
Email marketing Platform - Monthly fee for basic to Force24	On-going	N/A	$300 x 12	To be added by you
Software packages - Typical CRM system ACT!	From $20 per user per month	N/A	From $20 per user per month	To be added by you

Trade Shows - Booth 5 x 3 meters Transport/ logistics Misc. costs	One per year	Own labor $4,000 $1,500 $1,200	With agency support add $1,500	To be added by you
Admin Labor - Marketing Executive	1 x Inc taxes FT	$30,000 per YR	N/A N/A	To be added by you
Telesales	1 x Inc taxes PT	$15,000 per YR		
Miscellaneous marketing support - YouTube Videos	1 per month	Your time to complete Your time to complete	$8,000 Per YR	To be added by you
Photography	1 lot per month		$5,000 Per YR	To be added by you

It should be noted that many of these figures are ballpark because labor will vary around the world with places like Australia being more expensive and in the UK ditto in the South.

In addition, if you decide to outsource a lot or all of the work to an integrated marketing agency like mine, many providers, like Allott and Associates, will offer a package which will be cheaper than the agency completing just some of the individual marketing components.

Key points and actions you need to take from this chapter

1 - Although mind numbing, keeping a grip on marketing costs will help your business to correctly quantify whether to outsource or complete tasks in-house

2 - There can be some significant investment costs that need to be recovered as part of integrated marketing (although these would be more expensive if you performed the same tasks without integrating them) which is why ongoing monitoring is needed

3 - It is recommended that 8% of sales turnover is re-invested into marketing, however this pre-supposes that the margins on your product or service can afford this level of expenditure

4 - The budget works on what a typical SME might spend and will need reviewing and scaling back or up depending on the turnover of your business

Chapter 27

When things go wrong, how to get your marketing back on track

Integrated marketing works to a very successful tried and tested formula that has been developed by the author over 25 years. As you will have discovered each chapter talks about a specific specialist marketing component which links with the other deliverables. The aim as previously highlighted is to get two or even three deliverables out of each specific marketing task. The challenge of course with this type of approach is when things go wrong and your marketing gets knocked off course, because one marketing component is likely to affect at least one other and possibly more marketing deliverables.

As with all marketing things will go wrong and it is useful at this stage to explore some of the potential issues and then move on to get things back on track.

At this point you need to be really honest with yourself, have you done everything advocated in accordance with integrated marketing? The chances are you may have ignored some of the marketing components, whilst this is understandable it is vital that you do the heavy lifting such as database selection, pre-qualify contacts, emailing, phoning and using the other marketing tools to keep communicating with prospective customers. Remember typically, seven touches are required to remind potential customers of your existence before they fully engage.

The follow-up diagnostics question is whether your company has taken enough care in identifying your target B2B customer base and is the base large enough to deliver in the short to medium term the sales required? For a marketing campaign to be sustainable, ideally at least 100 companies at any one time, need to be directly targeted with intervention marketing through the likes of phone calls. In order to maintain this, an outer core of at least 1,000 companies is required to enable targeting over a period of time, which means that a full potential B2B audience should be around 10,000 companies. One of the reasons B2B marketing can go wrong is that companies run out of potential customers. If this sounds like you, go back to chapter four and see if you can identify further potential customers in adjoining sectors, but please don't forget that sloppy data kills sales, so your targets need to be in keeping with the Goldilocks Solution (see chapter four).

It is likely that you will be implementing integrated marketing with other staff members and possibly some external suppliers. Have you put in place KPIs concerning their deliverables? If not please do so as soon as possible. Also reiterate that the overall aim of integrated marketing is to try and galvanize everyone around the objectives. Whilst others may not share your passion, they should feel some motivation when things go right and some slight pain when things go adrift, as this will encourage them to provide greater commitment.

Are your marketing messages clear about what you want your audience to do?

The message across all communication platforms and for that matter the sales team, needs to be consistent, built around three powerful persuasive reasons why your potential customers should engage with the products and/or services your business is marketing.

Have you completed your competitor research and teased out why your offering is better? This could hinge around marginal items such as better service, improved product or even more knowledgeable staff, see chapter 25 for further ideas.

Take a look at the digital side of integrated marketing, what is the level of engagement with digital mailer pieces, the website and social media? What's the open rate for the digital mailers?

If it is below 20% consider refreshing the narratives to secure a higher open rate. If the website traffic is good but it is not generating sales, the offering may need refining, you will be able to decide this from the bounce rate, via Google Analytics.

You may also want to think about undertaking some retargeting through LinkedIn, if you don't believe there are enough potential customer touches for those who have visited the website. Do also look at the level of engagement on social media, if it is completely flat more effort is needed to engage with your target audience, consider adding YouTube videos about your product or service (if you haven't done so already). Post these videos onto the other social media platforms and tweet as a hyperlink. Remember the best videos for creating marketing traction are those that share technical knowledge or useful information, rather than sales jargon!

Re-look at SEO to increase your website traffic through pushing your website to the top of Google results pages. Consider investing some money into Google Pay-Per-Click (PPC) as a short-term solution to boost sales.

What is the typical sales cycle for the goods and/or services you are offering? I raise this valid point because B2B marketing mostly has a longer sales cycle than in B2C and it could be that you are being slightly premature in judging the sales disappointing.

Finally, whatever happens keep calm and carry on. Whatever goes wrong, it can be managed. Take a little time to analyze what has gone adrift. Talk to your colleagues, then regroup, re-plan, re-energize and carry on!

Key points and actions you need to take from this chapter

1 - Do accept that things will go wrong, don't take it personally just put them right

2 - Be really honest with yourself, have you done everything

advocated in accordance with this book?

3   - Has your company taken enough care in identifying your target B2B customer base?

4   - Agree KPIs with your team concerning their marketing deliverables

5   - Are your marketing messages clear? If not review them

6   - Check the level of engagement on the website, social media and digital comms

7   - Consider investing some money into Google Pay-Per-Click as a short-term fix

8   - Are you being too optimistic? Check the sales cycle

9   - Keep a cool head, regroup, re-plan, re-energize and carry on!

Chapter 28

Making a start: how to get the campaign off to a flying start

Everything has a beginning - even the bible - which for some is the most exciting part of the integrated marketing journey. However, I hope that the majority of readers who are now reading this chapter have been on a voyage of discovery, to help them either better understand or grasp that the market for the majority of B2B sales is limited in size. The size of your potential market, unless you are selling banking, card machines, insurance or even stationery will typically vary in size from between a few hundred companies to tops 10,000 companies. Therefore, what you are supplying is likely to be niche. This is why integrated marketing is so important, making one marketing activity fulfil two or more marketing functions. The aim is simple: to eke out additional sales whilst keeping all the marketing costs sustainable.

The starting point of this journey is your potential customers, the people you would most like to reach. Some businesses take this part so seriously that they actually have a dummy to represent the customer, which sits in internal marketing meetings, so that reference can be made to the customer in order to retain focus. While I wouldn't necessarily advocate going this far, understanding your target customers is critical to your campaign's success.

If you have read some of the other chapters you will already know that until Amazon and Apple started engaging with customers, they had no idea what those customers wanted, but once they engaged with them and consulted them, they effectively never looked back. Research your existing purchasers and target new customers. Understand what your potential buyers do and try and model your product or service around them.

You will need to make some decisions concerning some of the aspects of the integrated marketing work needed, do you intend to do everything in-house or outsource certain parts of the campaign? This may not be as simple as it sounds because the chances are that you will need external help with graphics, the website, a digital communications platform like Force24 or support with PR writing and some parts of social media, so the chances are that you will need to work with some external suppliers. As a starting point draw up a list of potential suppliers, which is in the appendices, alternatively you could outsource everything to a specialist international agency like Allott and Associates.

If you are planning to do the work in-house, do you have enough staff, do they have the right skillsets and how much of your time, yes, your time do you plan to devote to delivering integrated marketing? The point at issue is whether you plan to recruit or find external suppliers like a PR, design and digital agency or freelancer to help you, unless you provide the leadership and push, nothing much will occur, whatever else does ensue do not let inertia take over otherwise integrated marketing just won't happen!

Establish accounts with the relevant social media platforms, some of these are free, at this stage we are talking just about Twitter, LinkedIn, Facebook and YouTube. It would be sensible to also set up a subscription with Hootsuite or one of its rivals so you can automatically post across Twitter, LinkedIn and Facebook at the same time, rather than individually and at random!

If you plan to use Force24 or one of its rivals for distributing marketing material you may need help with developing your storyboards such as the graphics and text, plus you'll need to set up an account with your automated marketing platform provider.

You will also need to decide whether changes to your website are needed, or if you require the building of a website if you are a start-up business. Just a word of caution here, if you are an existing business and you have an established website, which is relatively modern with responsive templates, don't get pressed into creating a completely new website (which will take time to settle in). Your current site may only need optimizing with a facelift and some SEO repositioning work, please read chapters seven and eight for more details.

Determine what are the key communication messages you want to put across as everything from the website to the PR needs to be in alignment, this is critical with integrated marketing otherwise you will end up with disjointed messages and wasted money. Invest some time and effort to complete the process, if you are stuck there is a whole industry out there that specializes in strategic alignment that would be happy, for a price, to spend a day or more supporting you.

Start work on preparing your marketing plan for the next 12 months. At this stage it can be in outline until you have decided on the final communications strategy, otherwise you could start making the strategy fit the marketing plan! The milestones that need including in your plan are pretty much fixed and should include any exhibitions you plan to display at, any forthcoming or regular product or service launches, forthcoming trade publication features that may only be covered once a year, internal business changes such as recruitment and structural changes in production and/or premises, plus finally any seasonal issues such as high or low demand at certain times in the year, which could impact on marketing. Pretty much all other changes can be accommodated in a timeframe to suit you.

The marketing plan needs to cover a year and preferably be aligned with your financial year. All plans have limitations, your limitations are governed by the risk the shareholders are prepared to take which will be reflected in the size of the marketing budget and the limitations in terms of the marketing vehicles available to reach your target audience.

Once the plan has been drafted consult with your colleagues and pick up on any changes they suggest as it is imperative that everyone buys into the plan. To support you I have included a suggested draft plan overleaf, please remember this is a generic plan and will require adaptations to fit your business.

It is easy to get so excited in the euphoria of the marketing planning that you can forget about ROI, how are you going to measure your investment? In chapter 25 concerning ROI, a matrix covers each marketing component to try and measure its individual performance, resulting in a final tally of the return. Replicate the same in the index of your plan so that you at least have in place some measures of expected return.

If anyone says marketing or integrated marketing can be made fully automated, they are selling you a pipedream. Whilst various marketing components can be automated, at the moment the technology to link everything together is missing.

Having agreed your plan, put in place your internal team (this might just be you), agree your marketing support partners, you are now in a position to venture out and start the marketing campaign. Try and keep your plan reasonably flexible, although you will need to work to the timeframes agreed during the first quarter. Once you are towards the back part of the first quarter, you will need to decide what is working and to review what is not working. At this stage don't be too harsh on yourself or the integrated marketing plan you have put in place. Revise and if necessary, refocus because integrated marketing will only work if there is a suitable market to sell to. Just like in gardening if you plant seeds on unfertile wasteland you are unlikely to see a bumper crop. Getting your plan to work perfectly will take many months of fine tuning so please do stay focused on getting the best possible results. Do celebrate your successes and don't take any failures too personally. Remember getting things right can take years, although I would like to believe that by following the guidance of this book you should short circuit many of the obvious pitfalls.

At this point in the book I would like to remind you of Colonel Sanders, famous for the creation of the fast food chain KFC. Sanders had various jobs including engine stoker, lawyer, salesman, ferry boat owner and lamp manufacturer. Due to various setbacks including the depression, his early business ventures did not work out. Undeterred he eventually started selling fried chicken at a roadside restaurant which resulted in him perfecting a secret formula for pressure frying chicken, which he subsequently patented. At the age of 62, after visiting restaurant after restaurant who all declined his business proposals and sometimes sleeping in the back of his car to keep costs low, he eventually successfully got restaurants to buy into his formula and subsequently founded a franchise operation. Today KFC is in 150 countries and has in excess of 20,952 KFC outlets.[1]

Whilst I would like to believe that your integrated marketing success will flow in months or at worse perhaps a year, never forget the likes of Colonel Sanders who never gave up and after decades of failure eventually became a multimillionaire.

What I am saying ladies and gentlemen is don't be afraid of failure, because at this point the worst thing you can do is do nothing!

Your Company – Integrated Marketing Plan

1 - January – March

Promotional Theme – Reaching core market one:
Opportunities: communicate with a segmented core marketing and ensure that the key players are aware of your company and what it offers.

Databases:

Purchase suitable database from Selectabase or comparable based on 100 – 2,000 names.

Telesales:

Research to find relevant contacts and email details;

Create and send introductory email via Force24;

Follow-up within 24 hours;

All sale leads to be passed to the sales team immediately.

E-marketing:

Create storyboards and digital email flyers as part of the marketing touches;

Email each contact with a personalized email up to six times via Force24 or comparable supplier;

Monitor web page open rates and contact companies that click into the website.

Website:

Create relevant, on page content to match the quarter's marketing themes;

Optimize the core pages of the website within the first week of the campaign;

Add latest news content, including Google Analytics and Force24 tracking software.

Editorial:

Submit 2 x press releases relevant to monthly theme;

Produce 1 x case study concerning a past contact;

Create 1 x general feature article aimed at trade publication relevant to the theme.

Social Media:

Upload 5 work day tweets per week, search for new followers;

Update the LinkedIn page and ensure regular weekly postings;

Update Facebook post daily (can be automated via Hootsuite).

YouTube footage relevant to the monthly theme for posting on the website, sending to potential customers, uploading to YouTube and embedding as a link in the e-newsletter.

Quarterly e-newsletter:

Design based on a four-panel newsletter encompassing news, past case studies, features and other company content.

Other Marketing Activities:

Monthly review meeting to monitor activities against the plan;

Consider Google Ads to support the theme and any relevant on page advertising;

LinkedIn retargeting advertising for people who visited the website;

Look at an exhibition that you may wish to provisionally book;

Regularly capture photographs to support the theme for PR, website and social media;

Check branding is consistent across all platforms and marketing activities;

Check everything is in integrated alignment.

Subsequent quarters will follow an updated version of the first quarter's plan, remember your plan is all about grinding out marketing opportunities, it doesn't have to be sexy but it does have to be thorough, otherwise you will not create the marketing openings your sales team need.

Key points and actions you need to take from this chapter

1 - The starting point is your potential customers; make sure you have done your research

2 - Decide on your suppliers and what you are doing in-house

3 - Create accounts with the various platform providers like

Twitter, LinkedIn etc

4 - Check that your website is fit for purpose and can easily be updated or optimized to fit with your quarterly promotional themes

5 - Start writing your marketing plan segmented into quarters

6 - Be flexible and if you only have limited success concentrate on the things that are working, don't take failure personally

7 - Finally don't be afraid of failure as the worst thing you can do is to do nothing!

1 https://rlist.io/l/countries-with-the-most-kfc-restaurants-

Chapter 29

Motivation is the key to successfully implementing integrated marketing

Now is the time to mentally prepare for that integrated marketing battle that lies ahead. You should by now understand the different marketing components, have completed your market research, prepared a financial budget and a marketing plan, broken down by months and quarters for the next 12 months, in fact the only remaining barrier is your motivation to deliver it.

You know from the last chapter what you need to do and you need to start that journey now. No buts or excuses as you can't afford to delay, because only you can make it happen.

I want you to think, indeed believe, that you are a famous leader, your troops are roused but only you can bring that final piece of motivation, they are looking to you, yes you, to provide the leadership. This, reader, is the difference between a true leader and a bystander. The bystander is never around when things get bumpy but a true leader is there through thick and thin. A true leader has a strategy, in your case integrated marketing, and it's a battle, a battle to be conquered and only you can deliver the victory.

Throughout history men and women have had to stand up to tyrants or be conquered. You now have a choice, you can either be ruled by your old marketing methods or you can break free and go in a new bold direction, but ultimately as you are a free spirit, only you can make that decision. So, what are you going to do - call it? Or make excuses, shying away and leaving it to others to take up the challenge? You are at the bar of history; you can change everything at your company and make it happen. You can now develop your company, reward yourself and enrich the lives of your employees, by dramatically increasing the marketing reach and performance of the business, but remember only you can deliver it.

When things get tough at work which they do in any business, I sometimes remind myself of Winston Churchill. In 1940 Churchill was a 66-year-old newly installed Prime Minister, who following the fall of Dunkirk awaited the Germans amassed at Calais ready to invade. All UK churches were told to ring their bells to alert people when the invasion started and there were even some in his Cabinet, like Lord Halifax, who wanted to negotiate a surrender. Despite being older than the retirement age, he gave one of the greatest speeches in history; here is an extract: "... we shall fight on the beaches, we shall fight on the landing grounds, we shall fight in the fields and in the streets, we shall fight in the hills; we shall never surrender, and even if, which I do not for a moment believe, this Island or a large part of it were subjugated and starving, then our Empire beyond the seas, armed and guarded by the British Fleet, would carry on the struggle, until, in God's good time, the New World, with all its power and might, steps forth to the rescue and the liberation of the old." This speech along with others helped to unite the British people and to ultimately win the Second World War. The speech paved over the fact that the British army had just been rescued at Dunkirk by the most irregular navy in history and had to leave behind vast amounts of new equipment including tanks.

Churchill succeeded in uniting a Cabinet, country and what is now the Commonwealth. All you need to do is show leadership and deliver integrated marketing. Statistically your odds on delivering it are vastly superior to those of Churchill in 1940, who incidentally slept with a gun under his pillow, so what's stopping you delivering?

I appreciate you may have self-doubts, I also sometimes have them but the answer is to plan, plan and plan and then with a steady hand deliver, deliver and deliver.

Listen to what Muhammad Ali, an American professional boxer, activist, and philanthropist says: "Impossible is just a big word thrown around by small men who find it easier to live in the world they've been given than to explore the power they have to change it. Impossible is not a fact. It's an opinion. Impossible is not a declaration. It's a dare."

What I am asking you to do is not classed as impossible; it is relatively easy, if you are motivated.

John F. Kennedy in his famous oath of office as the 35th President of the United States said: "And so, my fellow Americans: ask not what your country can do for you — ask what you can do for your country. My fellow citizens of the world: ask not what America will do for you, but what together we can do for the freedom of man."

If I told you that if every company selling B2B in the UK, North America, Australia and New Zealand adopted integrated marketing and it increased their productivity by 5%, this would add around $6,000 to the annual wage packet of their employees,[1] don't you owe it to your fellow employees to deliver integrated marketing?

Of course, you may be concerned about the work integrated marketing might create. Well that's not necessarily true because once set up, using a mapped out plan as highlighted in the earlier chapter, you should have more time available to handle the increased number of sales enquiries you have generated.

To get things moving you need to be motivated, don't put off starting your campaign until tomorrow or next week, next month or even next year. Agree a start date for when the campaign should start and work to your pre-agreed timetable. Yes that might be tough, if you are feeling unwell, but at least you can feel sure secure in the knowledge you have chosen the day, be the victor not the victim!

Many people have to overcome adversity. Australian Nick Vujicic, 36, was born without any limbs and struggled early on in his life. Today he is a top performing motivational speaker. Vujicic who is now married with four children, turned what was his disadvantage into a USP marketing point. At school he was bullied but sought refuge in Christianity, by telling people it was God's plan so he could inspire other people. After giving a TV interview in 2008 he has taken the speaking circuit by storm. You most likely don't have to overcome the prejudices and bullying that Vujicic has suffered, so if Vujicic can motivate the world surely you can motivate yourself and others to make it happen.

Motivation is a critical word because your drive to make things happen will inspire others, perhaps slightly less motivated, to rally to raise the flag.

Having motivated yourself your next task is to motivate your employees. Many people in history have had to rally people often in very adverse conditions. In 1588, Queen Elizabeth I of England spoke to her troops in preparation for the arrival of the Spanish Armada, stating: "I know I have the body of a weak, feeble woman; but I have the heart and stomach of a king, and of a king of England too, and think foul scorn that Parma or Spain, or any prince of Europe, should dare to invade the borders of my realm; to which rather than any dishonour shall grow by me, I myself will take up arms, I myself will be your general, judge, and rewarder of every one of your virtues in the field."

I suspect there was not a dry eye in the audience, but the key point to note is that her troops were motivated and therefore willing to, if necessary, die to defend her England.

Motivating employees and/or third-party providers is key to getting things done because even if you are motivated, if others do not share your vision for integrated marketing it may never happen. Of course, whilst for most businesses, implementing integrated marketing is not a do or die solution, speaking from the heart with some reasoned arguments to supporting staff will normally win over even the more skeptical employees.

A chief executive at a business I worked at nearly 30 years ago, thought he knew better and once told me to draw a line on the floor and to ask those who were with me to cross it. I tactfully asked what I did with anyone who didn't cross the line but he simply looked scornfully at me, sadly he was fired just after that for underperformance!

Motivating people is not about drawing lines on the floor but all about winning them over and then keeping them on message, you can tell people what to do but it is much better management to explain what you are looking to achieve and then enthuse them. However, don't be fooled in believing that enthused people always stay on message, review your integrated marketing with them at weekly and more formal, monthly intervals, give them feedback, give them encouragement and praise their achievements.

So reader, if you are motivated, your team are motivated and you have your integrated marketing plan, what are you waiting for? It's time for you to deliver!

It is my pleasure and duty to stop driving you on this important marketing journey and to throw down the gauntlet so you can take up the challenge. Please stay true to the marketing processes articulated in this book, because now is your time to deliver integrated marketing, your day has now dawned.

As Chinese philosopher and writer Lao Tzu says: "Do the difficult things while they are easy and do the great things while they are small. A journey of a thousand miles must begin with a single step."

No excuses, just get on with that marketing transformation now!

Key points and actions you need to take from this chapter

1 - To implement integrated marketing you need to be motivated, look at how others have had to overcome adversity to be successful

2 - Don't be afraid of change; see it as an opportunity for the greater good of the business and your employees

3 - Take ownership, understanding that the delivery of integrated marketing rests with you

4 - Agree a start date and stay true to the program

5 - Motivate your employees and subcontractors, share your vision, enthuse them and give them recognition when they help deliver integrated marketing

6 - Your day has now dawned; it is time for you, yes YOU to deliver

1 https://www.theguardian.com/business/2019/jul/05/uks-dire-productivity-growth-costing-workers-5000-in-lost-earnings

About this Book

The overall aim of the title *Integrated Business to Business Marketing* is to provide a practical hands-on structured marketing blueprint, that the average aspiring or already successful business reader can confidently use without needing to reinvent the wheel. At the end of each chapter is an action list and checklist allowing anyone, even those with a limited attention span, to deliver tangible results. The book is written relatively jargon free, as the author does not believe he needs to justify his own importance or try and make marketing for the average reader unnecessarily fraught.

Understanding what needs to be done to get good results, without spending a king's ransom or burning the midnight oil to generate those sales, is at the very heart of what *Integrated Business to Business Marketing* is about. Whether the reader is an established enterprise or business start-up, *Integrated Business to Business Marketing* has been written to provide a complete marketing blueprint.

Integrated Business to Business Marketing is broken into a series of interlinked chapters which inform the reader with the actions and effort needed. Where possible a recognized and motivational quote is provided at the start of each chapter.

At the center of the book is a perpetual marketing wheel. This has been pioneered by the author and is a key part of the book's promotional philosophy, based on structured marketing. In a nutshell the case study that was written and issued last month becomes the Twitter and Facebook feed, e-newsletter content and the basis of the targeted email shot to similar prospective customers. Whilst this might sound simple the majority of SME companies, visited by the author, either don't have a cohesive marketing plan or do the different marketing functions separately, leading to garbled marketing messages, duplicated effort, wasted funds and often poor results.

Integrated marketing involves firstly, identifying appropriate companies to target and then making the different promotional components work together rather than in isolation.

The book is predominantly aimed at SME firms, which represent over 98% of all companies in the US, Canada, UK and Australia, who wish to promote products or services to other businesses or want to understand how to do so.

In the history of the world there have never been as many different marketing channels with which to communicate a promotional message as there are today. Email, Facebook, Twitter, LinkedIn, e-newsletters, direct mail, phone canvassing, websites and public relations may be the most obvious choices, but what about permission marketing, website retargeting through LinkedIn, digital advertising and newly emerging digital technologies like user traceable cookies?

In an advanced digital era, with data available on almost everyone and everything, knowing how to bring these different technologies together into a cost-effective integrated marketing strategy that works to create new business sales is paramount to the success of any firm.

This book builds on the author's thirty years' experience of successfully implementing marketing programs in the UK, mainland Europe, the US, Canada, South Africa and Australia.

About the author

The author has been involved in business to business sales and marketing since the age of 21, enabling him to build on over 39 years of real experience. In his previous employment he helped launch the Amstrad range of microcomputers into UK businesses and was directly involved in subsequently introducing Schneider Computers to the UK. In 1993 following Black Wednesday, he established his own marketing agency, Allott and Associates Ltd, and still remains its chairman.

Allott and Associates Ltd, with offices in London and Yorkshire, is a leading niche provider of business-to-business marketing services to companies based in the US, Canada, Australia mainland Europe and the UK. Through work undertaken for numerous clients Philip has been instrumental in delivering successful marketing programs for a cross-section of companies ranging from SMEs to PLCs.

Philip's work on numerous PR and marketing projects has equipped him with a deep understand of how to cost effectively deliver successful outcomes, knowledge which he has subsequently used to write this book.

Whilst establishing his marketing agency, Philip also took a law degree in Leeds, graduating in 1997. His dissertation was at the heart of the Brexit changes that took place in the UK during 2020.

A former regional chairman of the Federation of Small Businesses and fellow of the Chartered Institute of Management, he is the author of numerous business marketing reports, papers, media material and is also the published author of *The Donkeyman*, a gripping book about the life and times of his father.

From the author

Thank you for purchasing Integrated Business to Business Marketing which I sincerely hope supports your marketing journey, no matter when it started or where you are located.

I have enjoyed sharing my knowledge in the desire that it will help fellow marketeers, business executives and directors with both campaign direction and motivation. Remember marketing is the heart of any successful business and if it is wrong the whole enterprise not just the marketing could be put in jeopardy.

If you can spare just a few minutes, please do add your review of this book to your favorite online site for feedback and to help me and the team at John Hunt Publishing. Also, if you would like to connect with me and my other forthcoming books, please visit my Facebook site Integrated Business to Business Marketing - for more news.

Index

Appendices

Potential suppliers

ACT!	https://www.act.com
Allott and Associates	https://www.allottandassociates.co.uk
Creditsafe (UK)	https://www.creditsafe.com
Dun & Bradstreet	https://www.dnb.com/contact-us.html
Force24	https://www.force24.co.uk
Google Ads	https://ads.google.com
Harvest (US + Aus + NZ)	https://harvestbc.us
Hootsuite	https://hootsuite.com
D&B Hoovers	https://www.dnb.com/products/ marketing-sales/dnb-hoovers.html
Kompass	https://www.kompass.com
LinkedIn	https://www.linkedin.com
OnePoll	https://www.onepoll.com
PRmax	https://www.prmax.co.uk
Selectabase (for UK B2B/ B2C data)	https://www.selectabase.co.uk

SEMrush	https://www.semrush.com
Squarespace	https://www.squarespace.com
Facebook & advertising ads	https://www.facebook.com/business/
Travail Employment Group	https://www.travail.co.uk/
WordPress	https://wordpress.com
YouTube account	https://www.youtube.com

BUSINESS
BOOKS

Business Books

Business Books publishes practical guides
and insightful non-fiction for beginners and professionals.
Covering aspects from management skills, leadership and
organizational change to positive work environments, career
coaching and self-care for managers, our books are a valuable
addition to those working in the world of business.

15 Ways to Own Your Future
Take Control of Your Destiny in Business and in Life
Michael Khouri
A 15-point blueprint for creating better collaboration, enjoyment,
and success in business and in life.
Paperback: 978-1-78535-300-0 ebook: 978-1-78535-301-7

The Common Excuses of the Comfortable Compromiser
Understanding Why People Oppose Your Great Idea
Matt Crossman
Comfortable compromisers block the way of anyone trying to
change anything. This is your guide to their common excuses.
Paperback: 978-1-78099-595-3 ebook: 978-1-78099-596-0

The Failing Logic of Money
Duane Mullin
Money is wasteful and cruel, causes war, crime and dysfunctional
feudalism. Humankind needs happiness, peace and abundance. So
banish money and use technology and knowledge to rid the world
of war, crime and poverty.
Paperback: 978-1-84694-259-4 ebook: 978-1-84694-888-6

Mastering the Mommy Track
Juggling Career and Kids in Uncertain Times
Erin Flynn Jay
Mastering the Mommy Track tells the stories of everyday working
mothers, the challenges they have faced, and lessons learned.
Paperback: 978-1-78099-123-8 ebook: 978-1-78099-124-5

Modern Day Selling
Unlocking Your Hidden Potential
Brian Barfield
Learn how to reconnect sales associates with customers and unlock
hidden sales potential.
Paperback: 978-1-78099-457-4 ebook: 978-1-78099-458-1

The Most Creative, Escape the Ordinary, Excel at Public Speaking Book Ever
All The Help You Will Ever Need in Giving a Speech
Philip Theibert
The 'everything you need to give an outstanding speech' book,
complete with original material written by a professional speech-
writer.
Paperback: 978-1-78099-672-1 ebook: 978-1-78099-673-8

On Business And For Pleasure
A Self-Study Workbook for Advanced Business English
Michael Berman
This workbook includes enjoyable challenges and has been designed to help students with the English they need for work.
Paperback: 978-1-84694-304-1

Small Change, Big Deal
Money as if People Mattered
Jennifer Kavanagh
Money is about relationships: between individuals and between communities. Small is still beautiful, as peer lending model, microcredit, shows.
Paperback: 978-1-78099-313-3 ebook: 978-1-78099-314-0